THE NEW BALLET

The New Ballet
Kurt Jooss
and his work
by A. V. Coton

Dennis Dobson, Ltd, London
1946

FIRST PUBLISHED IN GREAT BRITAIN IN 1946 BY

DENNIS DOBSON LIMITED
29 GREAT QUEEN STREET
KINGSWAY · LONDON WC2

This book is set in 10-pt. Plantin, a type-face named after Christopher Plantin, the Antwerp printer who produced the Polyglot Bible, a work outstanding both in scholarship and typography. Plantin is believed to have been designed by Granjon but was extensively used from 1555 by Christopher Plantin from whose specimen book it was revived by the Monotype Corporation in 1913. As the letters of Plantin are more closely linked than those of almost any other type, it is easy to read and reproduces well on any kind of paper. The following firms have contributed to the production of the book: *Composition and make-up* by MONOTYPING SERVICE LTD., London, E.C.4; *blocks* by NOAKES BROS. LTD., London, E.C.4; *dress-designs in eight-colour offset* by THOS. FORMAN & SONS LTD., Nottingham; *letterpress section* by WHITEHILL (PRINTERS) LTD., Birmingham; *photographic art section* by A. & E. WALTER LTD., London, E.C.2; *binding* by DOW & LESTER LTD., Luton, Beds. The following artists have contributed to the production of the book: *Layout and typography* by JOHN HEARTFIELD; *drawing on binding* by DMITRI BOUCHENE; *jacket* by DORIS ZINKEISEN.

CONTENTS

Dedicated to the dancers of the Ballets Jooss—

Past, Present, and to come.

LIST OF ILLUSTRATIONS

COLOUR PLATES

The original dress designs, used in various ballets, are reproduced in eight colours

DRAWINGS

All line and pencil drawings in the book are by Richard Ziegler. The pencil sketches on pages 1, 10, 36, 40, 44, 50, 51, 64–5, 70, 156, and throughout the photographic section, were made during performances and rehearsals, often in the dark.

They often served as ' shorthand notes '—as the artist calls them—for the finished studio drawings on other pages. The favourite technique for their production is the duplicating stencil as the direct medium for his work. The endpapers, *The Dance of Death* and *The Dance of Life*, were produced in the same way, the background being printed through a sheet of tissue paper.

In the photographic section the drawings illustrate the artist's impression of the respective ballet with a few exceptions.

PHOTOGRAPHS

The photographs are a reflection of the development of the Ballets Jooss. Taken by several hands, the place and date have been given where known. Many of the photographs—including all those by Mr. Roger Wood—are action photographs. The photographs are in the following order :

PREFACE

HIS book is an attempt to record one of the significant artistic achievements of this century in the European Theatre—the creation of a completely new method of theatrical dance. This method results from the analytical and creative ability of one man, Kurt Jooss. It has significance because it is the only method by which dance-works identifiable as Ballet have been created outside the idioms and ideologies of the older Classical Ballet. These dance-works have competed on level terms with the products of the established system for twelve years now, in European and American theatres, and are therefore a solid theatrical establishment. From these considerations, and in the light of a number of years interest in, and occupation with, theatrical dancing, it seems to me that any further growth in the art of Ballet in this century will require that a good deal of the thinking and the technical innovations of Jooss should be grafted on to the Classical Ballet's method.

The two forms are in many senses complementary, though neither in itself possesses every æsthetic quality that Dance in the Theatre could—and ought to—show. The simplicity and directness of Jooss's dance system suggest that it is closer to the idiom and the ideology of the earliest sorts of theatrical dancing, than is the traditional system as expounded through the mechanism of the Classical Ballet. If the Theatre is to be again as dynamic a factor of our culture as it was in Elizabethan days (and as the Soviet Theatre is to-day in Russian culture), the first condition must be a casting-off of that adoration of the Past concealed in the phrase " respect for tradition." For this is the inhibition that prevents our present-day Theatre from being what it undoubtedly could be, that is the dominant cultural expression of our civilisation in our day. Too much regard for tradition has been the self-imposed burden under which the Classical Ballet has laboured for at least the past hundred and fifty years. It is precisely because Jooss disregarded tradition and began his work outside the Classical Ballet method that the lessons to be learnt from his career can be so important in the shaping of the Ballet of the future. The first incentive towards studying the structure of theatrical dancing grew from his contact with Rudolf Laban, though the method is Jooss's own creation, moulded out of his and Laban's thought and research, and machined into precise shapes by his philosophy. Laban is one of the little-appreciated thinkers in the last fifty years of theatrical history ; it is probable that he will be reckoned as historically important as Delsarte, Appia and Stanislavsky.

The revival of interest in the flesh-and-blood Theatre, which has so noticeably expanded during the war years, presages a time later in this century when the Theatre may be our primary cultural instrument. Whatever might be the novel technical forms through which the arts of the Theatre could assist this process, it seems unlikely that the formula of the Classical Ballet, as practised to-day, would be a weighty influence. The work of Jooss suggests that wider extensions of both idea and idiom among all kinds of theatrical dancing are not only desirable, but inevitable.

In these pages comparisons with the traditional form of European theatrical dance (defined as the " Classical Ballet ") are inescapable. This is the system which has been dominant for so long, and whose special forms and usages are directly challenged by the work of Kurt Jooss. The interpretation of some trends in its development, and the assessments on certain major artistic figures are, of course, my own conclusions, and for which I am indebted to no other opinion or estimate.

The writing of this book has been made more pleasurable by the willing help given by all members, past and present, of the Ballets Jooss organisation with whom I have made contact. They have freely given information, frequently argued against my point of view, and have talked with enthusiasm and great sensibility about many kinds of theatrical dancing. I am happy to record my indebtedness to those two scholars, enthusiasts and critics of Dancing, Cyril W. Beaumont and Lincoln Kirstein ; for many points concerning the history of theatrical dance I have drawn upon a comprehensive list of their works, as their approach to the subject seems to me to balance enthusiasm with thinking, and their partisanships are on an encyclopædic scale. My thanks are particularly due to Kurt Jooss, Gabor Cossa (of the Ballets Jooss), Richard Ziegler and my publisher, for their co-operation and encouragement.

FEBRUARY, 1945.   A. V. C.

NOTE.—The name " Jooss " is pronounced Y-Ō-S.

9

I

THE BACKGROUND OF TWENTIETH CENTURY BALLET

RATHER more than thirty years ago Diaghilev's Ballet invaded and conquered Paris and London, and showed to the whole world the first flowering of a new growth in contemporary culture. For one of the first things that happened to Russian Ballet when it expanded into Western Europe was that it ceased to be Russian. When Diaghilev died in 1929 it could be perhaps narrowly described as Franco-Russian Ballet. The resurgence of 1932 and all that has happened since shows that for twenty years under his direction, Ballet both stimulated and drew from all the arts and half the sciences of the Western world, and so was properly describable as European Ballet.

There are many reasons, some apparently contradictory, explaining why this branch of Theatre has achieved in our time a world-wide popularity. But the events even of this century are inadequately recorded; the rapid and often seemingly disconnected happenings that mark the rhythm of Ballet's progress have made for misunderstanding and dissension as often as they have inspired interest and stimulated curiosity. Years hence we may have some explicit documentary which can enable us to relate to each other the various technical and inspirational departures. Only then will it be obvious that the art of Theatrical Dance has undergone more sweeping changes of idiom and idea in the past thirty years than it experienced in the previous three hundred years.

The arts continue only because their idioms and ideologies are constantly changing : the shifts of idiom usually moving through cycles of increasing technical complexity which suddenly refine out to a pristine simplicity. This movement denotes—not the wheel coming full circle again—but a progress along one complete segment of an infinitely extending spiral. Each rediscovery of the strength of the simpler basic technical forms happens when the artist is engaged on work inspired by his highest creative potential. The particular " content " to which he is giving expression is too enormous to be framed within the academic formulas which are his precedents—even those he has shaped for himself previously. In these cases the decorative dross that has formed on the surface, as it were, of the basic technical codes is swept away, and a new vision of Truth or Beauty is fixed in a framework wrought from the elements of the craft. The " content " has been strong enough to compel the artist—mostly subconsciously—to give an unusual degree of precision and clarity to the work, so that it will touch instantly the spirit of those for whom it is created : all men living and to come.

The changes in ideology are generally derived from the strongest philosophical and political ideas in the air during the periods in which the art is richly fructifying. These considerations apply to the art of Ballet as much as to any other, and the process can be analysed through a study of any period of Ballet's history in the light of the social trends, political systems and philosophies agitating the society within which that phase of the art occurred. (Certain major artists can, and do, reject the socially-imposed function of mirroring the beliefs, popular myths and superstitions of their day, but the art of Ballet has rarely known creators who worked on this high level.) This is to say no more than that Art holds up the mirror to Nature : though the reflected image may take some time to travel back to the point of projection, and, when perceived, may disturb rather than flatter.

We need to remind ourselves occasionally that this is the inescapable function of Art, for it brings us sharply into fresh awareness of the fact that the making and the appreciating of works of art are about the only worthwhile activities in which Mankind has so far indulged. For, leaving aside the uncertainties of metaphysical speculation, we gather from history that the pursuit of the arts (which include the art of thinking) is the only thing that has brought any positive good, at either first or second remove, to anybody ; every other activity has been in some degree destructive or anti-social. All the arts that grace the present dispensation of Man spring from styles of religious observance which, in different societies, evolved into differing types of Drama. The commonest expressive vehicle of the earliest drama is a dance-ritual. This ritual was the crowning expression of a communal experience of religious rites, and the first thing that all priests, magicians and medicine-men have done to mark off their difference from their more earthy fellows has been to invent an esoteric system of movement and gesture, and to wear symbolic garments. The Theatre has not yet moved too far away from its earliest and simplest forms.

The primary importance in theatrical happenings of Dancing, patterns of stylised movement and gesture, gives the strongest clue to the present-day popularity of Ballet. Even to the totally uninitiated, theatrical dancing in its most obvious forms and its simplest ideologic shapes is as explanatory and satisfying as a tribal dance depicting a battle, a hunt, a successful wooing or a good harvest is to a so-called primitive man. For it offers the same fascinations of ordered movement, recognisable rhythmic accompaniment, unusual uses of colour and shape in ceremonial garb of a high order ; and it binds together performers and audience in the sharing of an experience which is supernormal compared with the daily routine of the breadwinning task.

In comparison with certain other popular forms, such as the Cinema and Magazine Fiction, for instance, Ballet has, until now at least, preserved some amount of æsthetic integrity. It cannot be made in a few attractive formula patterns capable of mass-reproduction, and it is not a good commercial proposition. Only through these intrinsic conditions do its artists still retain a high degree of working freedom in the choice of subject-matter and technical means. Of the many reasons for its ascendancy as the most popular form of symbolic art in our time, only a few can now be discerned. Probably the most obvious is that it " rings true " in a way that most products of Stage and Screen to-day do not. This " ringing true " may derive, for the greater part of its new and expanding audience, from the fact that Ballet is not bound up in a narrow scheme of formula plots such as enmeshes nearly everything else in Theatre and Cinema to-day. Ballet does not have to tell a story ; when it does, there need not necessarily be a happy ending to it. It presents, in ways no other kind of visual spectacle can command, immediately obvious beauties of sight and sound imagery. The recipient is free to hang his own philosophic conclusions—which may vary with varying performances—on such works as " Lac des Cygnes," " Les Sylphides," " Choreartium," " Cotillon," " Horoscope." Its offering of plastic pattern, decorative painting, symbolic costuming, welded together in a time-and-space amalgam with music (which may or may not be tied down to a plot), has more possibilities for spontaneous emotional excitation, and at one remove, intellectual prompting, than any of the other art forms.

One evidence of the art's strength is the flexibility of the basic forms, and the wide range of impressions which can be conveyed through those forms. The classical theatrical dance of to-day, that is a type of Theatre encased in a movement-and-gesture style showing fairly continuous descent from Florentine and French dance spectacles of the late fifteenth century, can, to-day, give effective expression to all the mutations through which the art has passed in four hundred years. From Coralli's Romantic ballets, through the musico-dramatic lyrics of Petipa and Ivanov, the Fokine one-act moralities and dramas, the dance satires and plastic polemics of Massine, down to the traditional form's most interesting present-day trends—the musically inspired dance æstheticism of Balanchine and the astringent psychologic probings of Tudor—all this is based on a movement technique which has, by now, exploited to the full the visual physical potential of the performer.[1]

If the art is to continue, either as a separate form or in alliance with music-drama to create a fresh spectacular medium, it will only go on evolving through the applied results of the experiments made by its creative artists. These experiments involve a ceaseless overhauling and refining of technical means (and occasionally a rejection of all technical precedents) ; and the discovering of fresh ranges of ideas to be given expression. How this dual problem has been faced in the immediate past must be discussed briefly, and from a consideration of that evidence we can begin to assess the value of the work of Kurt Jooss. His contributions to the art of theatrical dance may be the most important single development in the growth of the art in this century . . . that is something that only Time will show.

We are still so close in time to Diaghilev that we have not yet gathered all the evidence of his activities. No

For notes refer to pp. 149-50.

definitive account of his manifold talents, and his usage of them, exists ; no one has yet produced that dispassionate and detailed record from which we can draw all the conclusions possible about what happened during his twenty years' exciting reign. At times his throne seemed to totter, and he consistently over-ruled his Cabinet when it suited him to do so. Yet from the shadows of the immediate past he already emerges as a person of multiple talents all successfully employed. He was the impresario who could conjure forth the needed millions, he was the artistic supervisor with a dead-right instinct for the moment's need, and he was the discoverer and exploiter of creative artists of every kind who could do work for Ballet. Certainly only through him was the choreographer placed at the top of Ballet's hierarchy, after a century at least during which the art had functioned as a mechanism for glorifying the ballerina. The re-adjustment whereby the parts of the producing mechanism fell into the new order of : first, the choreographer ; second, the choreographer's collaborators ; third, the choreographer's material, could only happen because of the existence of a creative artist of sufficient strength to shoulder the burden. The historic accident of timing which brought Diaghilev and Fokine together in the same place set out the essential conditions which made possible all the major developments in traditional Ballet from Fokine to Tudor. Even Diaghilev's particular genius could not have brought his venture to the success it achieved, had it not, at the start, been allied with the choreographic genius of Fokine. Fokine was the first of the great twentieth century choreographers, and by placing on him the ultimate artistic responsibility, Diaghilev inducted the era of the choreographers' domination. It is this new alignment of responsibility which has built the art to its present strength in the past forty years.

Fokine was no revolutionary, but he was a great reformer. He saw that Ballet nearly everywhere was stagnating, if not actually moribund. Although he questioned the old ideology and the creaking idioms through which it was expressed, his reforms were within the framework of the basic tenets then existing. He would make Ballet continue, as it had been throughout the past century, a decorative art-form, an escapist, rather than an invigorating theatrical experience, which would soothe the senses with devices of plastics-plus-music tied to a more grown-up fairytale than Perrot, Mazilier, Coralli or Petipa had generally used. He was to find the stories in legend, folklore and mythology, not exactly as his nineteenth century predecessors had done, but with the lore and mythology seen through the pink glow of *fin-de-siècle* optimistic philosophy. (In parenthesis one can say of Fokine, that though he had a far subtler appraisal of the æsthetic potential of classical Dance than, say, Perrot or Petipa, he was too conditioned by his social milieu to see it as anything else but an art for a rather soignée, intensely caste-conscious audience, who lived against a solid background of comfort and order, and had nicely developed cultural leanings towards France.)

He established in our time a hall-mark for Ballet : there is logic, completeness and individual style both in the choreography and in the method of interpretation required in each work. His formative influence on the whole choreographic craft lies in his freshly designed dance shapes, using on the whole the identical raw material that the previous age's choreographers had used, but applying it imaginatively. Further, he hammered into a more balletic style the existing folk-dance forms in common use and expanded their catalogue with Russian, Persian, mid-Asiatic and Eastern styles learned from travel, pictures, descriptions and research. Equally important was his re-shaping for contemporary use, *i.e.* to point the more fluent acting qualities *he* was introducing to Ballet, of the antique system of mime-gesture. Starting from the lush spontaneity of *commedia dell' arte*, this system had got lost somewhere in the dark forest of Romanticism, and when Fokine came to Ballet, he found it petrified into a group of quaint emphasis symbols which emphasised nothing to the modern audience but their own complete emptiness of meaning.

Much of his work is considerably dated when seen beside ballets of the half-dozen other choreographers who can be so classified in the same breath. There is apparently no contact with the world outside the Theatre since about 1914. But the works live, and will do so for long yet, not for their sympathy with, or even awareness of, the aura of this century, but because of their homogeneity. The homogeneous quality grows from their masterly exploitation of the widest range of dance movement available in the Theatre *up to that date*, and its union with a coherent style of acting such as Ballet had not previously compassed.

It was in consistency with Diaghilev's autocratic spirit and his artistic unscrupulousness that he should take every step to maintain his unique position. At the first disagreement over artistic control and the employment of other talents, he created a situation which compelled Fokine to resign. Nijinsky was the second choreographer, and, following so closely on Fokine, left works which have been on the whole harshly judged, and which, according to an unpublished authority, were not complete expressions of the enormous creative potential of Nijinsky. Had events moved in a different sequence between 1911 and 1914, he might have fixed a choreographic tendency as vivid and strong as anything we have seen from the other successors to Fokine. Although the latter artist returned later to Diaghilev's company, their association was completely severed by the outbreak of war. Throughout those four years the company was kept together by the manipulation of all Diaghilev's personal talents ; but it was kept in being, to launch the first ballets of Massine (before he was 21) in America, Spain and Switzerland. Massine was succeeded by, and in turn reinstated over, Bronislava Nijinska, in the middle twenties. By this time wavelets of dancers were allowed out of Russia into Western Europe, and from amongst them, in the person of Georgei Balanchine, was brought to light yet a fifth choreographer. Each of these creative artists, working at the very core of Ballet in a time when the turmoil of the century was forcing all the arts into commentative shapes, did something to change the ideology from that romanticism that had lain on it for so long. They guided its development, mostly unknowingly, into a kind of non-representational art such as Music and Painting had already become in the twentieth century.

By the time Diaghilev died, his Ballet had appeared in most of the big cities of Europe and America, and had brought about a revolution of ideas about Ballet wherever Ballet was still in existence as a living Theatre force. It had become a form capable of transmitting, and enriching, ideas about the contemporary scene : complementary to this process it had been the channel through which most of the creative enrichments in Stagecraft (particularly Lighting), Theatre Music, Decor and Costuming had come to the European Theatre. Though the company was to dissolve practically overnight at its founder's death, the artists associated with it were, within a very few months, to re-combine and continue the creation of Ballet on companies formed with the avowed intention, perhaps among many other intentions, of following in the master's footsteps.[2]

No ballet by Fokine (at least, as far as 1939) is on a contemporary theme, and few of them succeed in re-stating a myth or illuminating a poetic concept in terms of the theatrical dynamic informing such works as " Ode," " Choreartium," " The Green Table " or " Cotillon." But one cannot choose any work by any of Diaghilev's choreographers and say of it : That was the point at which the shift of balance came. One can only indicate the creations of the period 1909-1929, and note at a hundred different points the evidence of the transition that was taking place. The transition, not yet completed, was from pictorial stagecraft, story-telling and the ballerina-vehicle to a theatrical method giving high symbolic expressiveness to myths, æsthetic documentary and plastic pageantry. This slow crawl up a segment of the spiral has been chiefly motivated by the juxtaposition of five choreographers, a dozen or so superb dancers, and a handful of painters, poets and composers, all of whom were, in varying degrees, sensible of the spirit of the age and worked (to a considerable extent unconsciously) under Diaghilev's mesmeric spell. The work of these people undoubtedly saved the art from collapsing into the sterility it was gradually approaching in Russia. (Within Russia it has survived the rigours of several years of chaotic conditions following on the war and the revolution, only because the academic mechanism was strong enough to support a complete change of ideology : and up to 1917 it kept in existence only because it was lavishly funded from the Czar's pocket.)[3]

But the work of the Diaghilev organisation, valuable though it was, had not achieved everything. The technical enlargements of Fokine, the highly co-ordinated movement and colour rhythms expounded by Massine, and the sensitive plasticity with which Balanchine complemented the inner rhythms of the music he used—all these gave the form fresh theatrical vigour, enlarged its æsthetic effect. At the farthest point of advance, they showed that the art could be freed from the effects of the increasingly retrogressive romanticism that had overlain it since the days of Vigano.[4] Now, although its artists had thrown the art open to the influences working through all the strata of our civilisation (and as part of the process they had had to revise the traditional ideas about the extent to which Music, Painting and Theatrecraft could be welded with Dancing), they took for granted the absolute suitability of the classical ballet technique for their work. None of them seems to have questioned seriously the validity of that technique, or to have made any research into what might have been the most important question they could ask : Does the classical method of dance training utilise the dancer's body to 100 per cent. effectiveness ? The lack of this consideration influenced all their work.

Because it has been in existence for so long, changing bit by bit, but not reaching very far beyond the first codifications of Arbeau, Beauchamps, and Blasis, the classical technique is not necessarily the only effective basis for theatrical dance movement styles.[5] Several innovators have at various times, and in amazing ways, challenged this implied excellence. Only one man has created what is recognisably Ballet, in our time, working outside the traditional line of development—Kurt Jooss. The continuous existence of his work, and the growing interest in it, are due to its truly theatrical quality. Its theatrical truth is measured by its expressive richness, and this grows logically from a union of Form and Content which is based on a revaluation of the dancer's bodily potential. His teaching is rigorous, and is based on a system of physical co-ordinations more logical and with deeper-growing roots than the older system as expounded in Blasis' documentary—which is to-day the source book of the best traditional technical method. Kurt Jooss's method discounts, just as much as the other method does, the theatrical propriety of dance innovations as undisciplined (and therefore as unteachable) as those expounded by the prophets who have arisen to save the art of Dance from itself. He effects, in a theatrical atmosphere and setting, a synthesis of Music, Dance and Acting which flows into, and, at the same time, stems from, the material which is the expression of his ballets. In this he aims for the same objective towards which any other dance-creator is reaching ; with the difference that, to him, Content is always more important than Form, where the classical choreographer is frequently unable sufficiently to discipline Form, and permits it to define, and therefore considerably to colour, Content.

14

II

THE BIRTH OF THE BALLETS JOOSS

KURT JOOSS was born inside this century; by 1919 he had completed his high-school studies, and though yet undecided about a profession, he had undertaken the study of photography. A positive curriculum of something above " the three R's " was indicated, and in early 1920 he was enrolled a student at an outstanding musical academy—the *Württembergische Hochschule für Musik*—and also at a famous Stuttgart dramatic academy. The German Youth Movement, a powerful manifestation of education-through-culture, had been in existence since his schooldays, and his membership of this body channelled his deep and passionate interest in acting, music and dancing. This body, catering for that Heinean romanticism innate in this century's first generation of German youth, and fostering a passion for Greek athleticism and the open-air life, had a great resurgence after 1918, and tens of thousands of young people lived under far freer conditions than were then possible in any other form of society. They gathered at evenings, in week-ends and holidays, to read, discuss, act, dance, sing, play music, these activities being complemented with camping, climbing and tramping.

Shortly after engaging on his copious Stuttgart timetable, Kurt Jooss found a fascinating study in the production problems implicit in Wagner's music-dramas. It was in this period that he was introduced to Rudolf Laban, who was then living in Stuttgart. What Jooss had already discovered of the crafts of the Theatre inclined him to listen attentively to Laban's discourses on a theatrical subject—the artistic expressiveness of body-movement. By that time, Laban had been engaged for more than twenty years on research into, and a revaluation of, the Dance as a Theatre art.

Rudolf Laban had spent much of his early life in Bosnia, now a part of Yugo-Slavia. This part of the Balkans had long been an outpost of the old Turkish Empire, where Moslem culture had been imposed centuries previously on the indigenous population. He acquired a background of knowledge concerning more than one European cultural style; he had some comprehension of Asiatic and Byzantine influences, as well as the Italian and North European ideologies which had shaped the history of the plastic arts since the Renaissance. He lived in Munich where he studied painting, and was for some time resident in Paris, in which city he made a study of dancing. He had a questing mind : and they were not too common in the Theatre during the smug years at the turn of the century. His interest in problems of plastic rhythm, and pictorial harmony, as manifested in Dancing and Painting, led him to a close examination of the technical developments in theatrical dance in Europe. He was satisfied that the spectacle of theatrical dance as he saw it then (the time was a little previous to both Duncan and Fokine and, outside Russia, Ballet was at the depth of its decadence) was an unseemly one. Dancers in the Theatre moved by a system which negated half the possibilities of physical movement, and produced action patterns that had little either of beauty or expressiveness in them.

Kurt Jooss became one of a group of young men surrounding Laban, and found that the study of movement from basic impulses would probably supply the answers to many of the questions he was asking about contemporary trends in the Theatre of Music and Dance. He worked under Laban in the search for an anatomical code of principles (which should exist, but had not apparently ever been scientifically sought out). This code should be defined from an analysis of mind, nerve, and muscle co-ordinations, and would involve research into little-exploited fields of psychological and mathematical thought, in addition to a thorough examination of all the factors which have influenced the general trends of movement codes for theatrical use. It was not, at this juncture, an irrelevant notion that came to Jooss—of some day seeing in existence an academy of the arts placed in a rural setting. To some extent this vision was later realised when the Jooss-Leeder School of Dance, the fount of personnel for Ballets Jooss, was established at Dartington Hall. This is the community directed for over fourteen years by Mr. and Mrs. L. K. Elmhirst, and which formed a novel and successful experiment in co-operative rural living. Scientific farming, the production of furniture, textiles, timber ; a co-educational school, and academies of Music, Acting and Dancing, were organised and run with the best equipment and personnel within one vast country estate in Devonshire which employed in these manifold activities over eight hundred persons. Jooss in the early 'twenties set out to study large-scale farm management with some similar objective in mind a long way in the future. He comes of Württemberger farming stock, and there was a possibility that he might inherit the home farm. He left Laban and went to work in the country near Ulm, then, after his father's death, on the farm at Wasseralfingen for almost a year. At the end of 1921 he renounced any claim on the farm, and returned to work with Laban. He was student, chief assistant and one of the dancer models whom Laban used for his research in Stuttgart, then, later, in Mannheim and Hamburg during 1922 and 1923.

The Theatre in Germany was at this time probably the most progressive in Europe, yielding nothing to even the best contemporary achievements in Soviet Russia. It was better equipped technically than any Theatre in any other country, and under the Weimar regime occupied an honourable and decently subsidised function in the State machinery. The old capitals of the various dukedoms and electorates had always been a constellation of cultural centres, and had scarcely owed anything of their quality to the influence of a dominating metropolis. Of such well-integrated theatres, that of Münster was an outstanding example, with, as its Intendant, Niedecken-Gebhard, a powerful theatrical personality and a great revolutionary in the field of opera production. The organisation of this theatre allowed for a " producer of movement " who was not only a dance-arranger, but who exercised a control and supervision over the ways in which actors and singers disposed of themselves when on the stage. This was Kurt Jooss's first professional engagement in the Theatre. Here he founded his group the *Neue Tanzbühne* around a nucleus of Aino Siimola, Sigurd Leeder and F. A. Cohen. The other two dancers had also been Laban students. Leeder had, in fact, started his dance career in Hamburg with Laban, after having studied some time previously with a pupil of Laban's. He had been a not unsuccessful actor and designer, but found in Laban's teachings and experiments a compulsion strong enough to direct him permanently towards dancing for the rest of his career.

The *Neue Tanzbühne*, as a department of the Münster Theatre, was allowed a separate existence, and Jooss was enabled to continue his dance research through the agency of the group. The first Jooss ballet, " A Persian Ballet," was presented at a Modern Music Festival at Donaueschingen in 1924. During this period of the 'twenties there was held an annual Handel Festival at Göttingen under the artistic direction of the Münster Intendant, in which the *Neue Tanzbühne* was engaged. It was at this period that Hein Heckroth joined the Münster Theatre as resident stage designer, working fruitfully with both Niedecken-Gebhard and Jooss. Apart from these activities away from Münster, the Dance Group also toured the towns of Western Germany with their experimental works.

The need to examine again, and from closer quarters, the traditional method of theatrical dance led Jooss and Leeder to Paris, where they undertook an intensive course of study in the classical Ballet. From here they went to Vienna to study under teachers working against a different background. To continue the experimental work and gain theatrical experience, the two pioneered the notion of the male concert-dancer unsupported by a filling-out of traditional work, chorus makeweight and musical and scenic decorativeness. In a tour of small German and Austrian theatres and concert halls they appeared under the stark and uncompromising billing of " Two Male Dancers." During this period the infant *Neue Tanzbühne* was kept alive under the direction of Jens Keith, yet another of Laban's Hamburg students, and Aino Siimola, who was still working as leading dancer in the Ballet at the Münster Theatre.

16

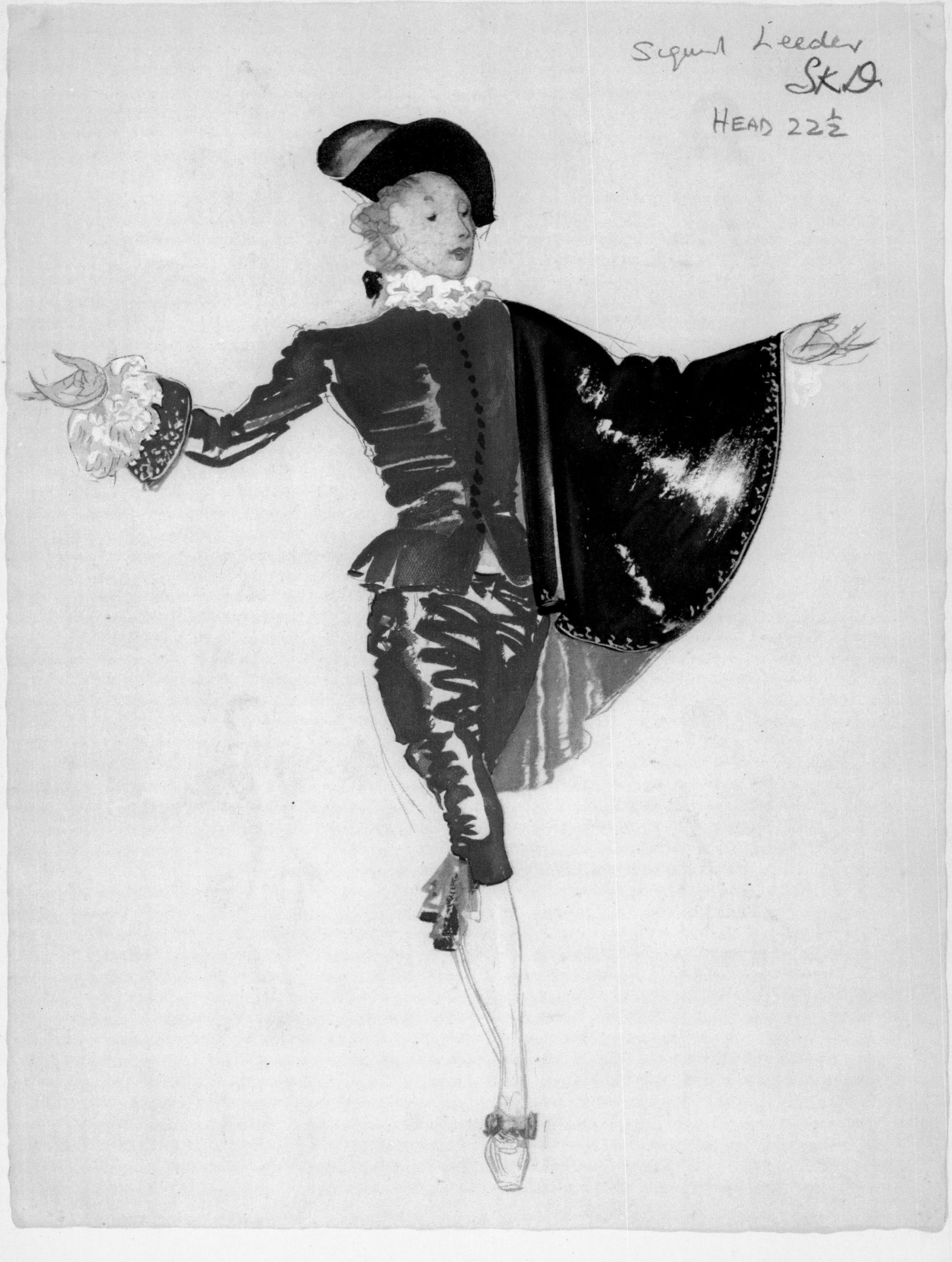
Sigurd Leeder
SKD
HEAD 22½

Micheal Chamley
SKB
HEAD 21¾"

Toschka Fedro
45008

flowers
2 rose buds

Spray twelve long
tight
roses & buds

spray 6" long
tight
roses & buds.

Ulla Soederbaum
45016
45017
(dyed taffeta)

6" spray

Haus Zullig SK-A
HEAD 22¼

22.

The town of Essen, in 1927, offered itself the civic satisfaction—not of widening its boulevards or of erecting statues and memorial halls to its famous citizens—but of founding a Theatre Academy, of whose dance section Jooss now became director, with Leeder as first assistant and collaborator in teaching. An All-Germany Dance Congress was organised shortly after the appointment, which was attended by the exponents of every academic and non-academic style that had arisen since Isadora Duncan blazed her trail across two continents. Every variety of Free Dancer, Expressionist, and Interpreter, as well as the personnel of the established Opera Ballets throughout Germany and the current ballerina of the Paris Opera, took part. Aino Siimola, who was now leading dancer at the Essen Opera, and F. A. Cohen, who had been producing Opera at Würzburg, resigned these posts and threw in their lots with Jooss. The academy at Essen was nominated the Central Laban School, and Jooss now acquired the office of ballet master to the Essen Opera House. For this work he employed those who had been the nucleus of the *Neue Tanzbühne*, and this grouping, which included students who had joined him after the removal to Essen, was the one on which he worked for a further four years before presenting in Paris " The Green Table."

Long before " The Green Table " burst on an unprepared dance public the work of Kurt Jooss had been building up slowly inside the Theatre. What emerged in the summer of 1932 was not merely the result of research and trial worked out in classes and rehearsal rooms, but an integrated style of movement whose first formulation had cost ten years' exacting work in the finest sort of dance-academy—theatrical performance before a cash-paying audience. Ten years after meeting Laban, Kurt Jooss had worked out a dance method which negated most of the premises that every ballet maker of this century had felt bound, in part at least, to accept. The biggest experiment to date was " The Green Table," which showed in a lengthy work, a complete denial of the alleged necessity for painted setting, corps-de-ballet as a decorative adjunct, and the colour range of orchestral accompaniment, as parts of a successful ballet. The company took this work to Paris for the *Concours Internationale de Chorégraphie* in 1932, and won a first prize of 25,000 francs for the most original composition. What resulted from this success was the establishment of " Ballets Jooss " to compare and compete with companies presenting works based on a method carrying five hundred years' tradition with it.

This Dance Congress had been organised by Rolf de Maré, formerly patron of the Swedish Ballet. Under the direction of Jean Borlin this company of Scandinavian dancers had produced works of Ballet comparable in integrity and adventurousness with the achievements of the Diaghilev enterprise. After Borlin's early death his friend and collaborator had instituted the Archives Internationales de la Danse, and the Congress was a logical outcome of this foundation. Rolf de Maré made it possible for dance works to be shown which might otherwise never have been seen in Paris. The lucid exposition, in " The Green Table," of the indecencies and inhumanities of warfare, together with the lack of any pretence that there is anything noble or superhuman about the process of mutual butchery, gave this work the impact of a thunderbolt. Form grew from Content in a manner rarely witnessed before in theatrical dancing ; and both the form and the expression underlined and enriched one another, in a style which was as dynamic as the material of the ballet's plot. The conferring of the award was followed by an offer to participate in a season of New Dance. The impresario concerned planned to make a new sort of theatrical attraction by showing the three prizewinners of de Maré's Congress. This novel bill was to be seen at the Casino de Paris during an autumn interval between two of the Casino's usual entertainments. When the Jooss dancers arrived in Paris, the plan had gone somewhat astray ; the Casino was continuing its revues, and neither of the other dance-groups was available. When the new autumn attraction opened, the typical Casino show of elegant nudity, risqué songs and even more risqué situations was followed, after the intermission, by the stark document of " The Green Table." The uproar, according to Jooss, was indescribable ; threats and insults were yelled at the dancers, jeering, screaming and whistling drowned the music so that Cohen conducted the dancers by gesture from his seat at the piano. This went on for several performances, but

the management persisted, so did Jooss ; by the second week the row had made " The Green Table " the most talked-of thing in Paris. A new and quite untypical audience began to visit the Casino, they approved the work, applauded and gradually wore out the opposition. In another week " The Green Table " had become acceptable.

A proper theatrical season in Paris was arranged for the next spring, after touring Holland, Belgium and Switzerland. In July the company paid its first visit to London, and the modest bill of works came fully into the limelight. The Ballets Jooss had established its right to dance a new kind of Ballet almost in the teeth of the resurrection then being effected for the Classical Ballet. For it was in this summer that the chief contestants for the mantle of Diaghilev, now four years dead, came into the ring together, these companies being " Les Ballets 1933 " and " Les Ballets Russes de Monte Carlo."

The appearance of Isadora Duncan on the dance stages of America and Europe was as important an incident in the history of Dance as the rising of the twin stars of Fokine and Diaghilev, which took place at almost the same time. They occurred exactly when the art of Dance was badly in need of reformers, visionaries and fanatics. Whilst Isadora began the first storming of the seemingly impregnable citadel of Ballet, Fokine and Diaghilev were making ready to transplant the art into Western Europe, while Europe was still able to provide a soil that could nourish it. And Fokine and Isadora met ; though how much she influenced him, in any way, it would be hard to say. In later life he had developed a fine contempt for anything of Dance that was non-balletic, but he did find her work natural, and with a congenital simplicity that must have been inspiring, in 1905. When they met he was in the full flush of his iconoclasm, and her outrageously unconventional work and the system of ideas behind it were a stimulation to the young man who knew he *had* to reform the theatrical dance of his time, or else turn his back on it for ever.

Isadora Duncan followed with a fine consistency the direction she had originally mapped for herself. Her starting point was from a simple belief that Dance is innate in all (which, considered from any angle, is a rather too obvious truism to be of much theatrical account in our mechanically over-ripe age). Her research was carried out on herself ; and from the premise that all movement arises at an inner source, which she called " the soul," and the corollary that the soul is located in the solar plexus, stemmed all her life work. She created moving personal translations of her soul-states into terms that were both visually and emotionally exciting. As a symbol she is stabilised—though not, historically speaking, a lone figure—as the pioneer of Dance freed from Tradition—of Dance as Expression—indeed, of Dance as anything else but the formalised concept which is Ballet.

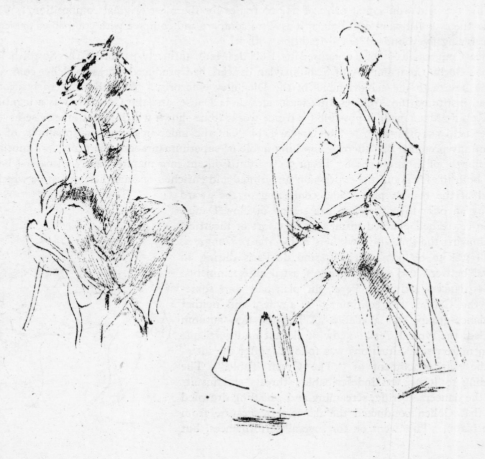

It is this symbolic figure with which very many people identify all the changes that have been wrought in forms of Dance in our time. Yet Isadora's basic idea is but one of many stimulants that have been injected into the corpus of theatrical dancing. Since her heyday, the whole pace and intensity of European life have changed, and the simple dogma that Duncan preached has, by now, been taken up, expanded, dissected, distorted and freshly coloured by several analyst-creators, and has been reborn in a dozen esoteric, and not necessarily exciting, forms.

Broadly, the whole of the researching into, and experimenting with, dance systems which reject the conventions of traditional Ballet, falls into two spheres of effort : the Middle European, and the American. Duncan was partly the instigator of both movements, though there is little left, in practice, of her methods. Even while she was leading her incredible caravan into the Olympian wilderness to set up a truly Grecian temple of the Dance, Ruth St. Denis in America was already creating a form of dance spectacle which established its theatrical validity very quickly. Her technical method seems to have been a tireless and candid application of Delsarte's felicitous expressionism to themes which she discovered in a study of the more exotic religions. Her association with Ted Shawn, a frankly gymnastic stylist, produced an academic method through which hundreds of young Americans were set dancing in the first thirty years of the century. The bloom of Denishawn lay on the surface of every Free Dancer in America, until the teachings of Laban set up effects which were ultimately felt on the far side of the Atlantic.

It is necessary to remind ourselves that this Modern Dance is as inevitable a development of the contemporary theatre as the Stagecraft reformation which, spreading over about fifty years, reached its zenith in the 'thirties. The particular moulding of both the modern German and the modern American temperament produced conditions in these two countries throughout the inter-war period which made them the inevitable milieux for so much dance experiment. In America much of the work has been in response to a subconscious need to establish inside that culture a modern humanistic philosophy. A different sort of conditioning gave incentive to the movement in Germany, though it can reasonably be claimed that had Laban not laid out the ground-plan, and done much of the essential research into First Causes of Movement, the European contribution to Modern Dance styles would lack the richness and variety that it at present shows.

The difference between the two creative trends lies in the fact that, whereas the Europeans felt their way towards a theory of plasticity, which would support and give shape to their philosophisings (with Laban standing in the centre, as it were, ready to show them the workings of the magic machine) —the Americans, placing the accent on individuality, developed a whole congregation of personal stylists who have not yet made contact with a central fund of ideas about their technical raw material. The one sphere of effort has been centripetal, and the other centrifugal ; and this tendency, in each case, exactly conforms with the general psychological characteristics of the social background giving rise to each of the movements.

To all alike in the beginning came the compulsion to establish *their* dance-form freed of any compromise with the traditions of the established theatrical Ballet. The pity was that so much of the work was lost because the executants required their audiences to swallow whole the new concept of Dance—raw Dance, unhampered by stage decoration, beautifying costume, and, in many cases, even the use of musical pattern. In this they betrayed their lack of that theatre-consciousness which has never been absent in Laban, Jooss, St. Denis, Graham, and a few others. For, once the idea enters, for a single moment, that the dance created is to be more than just a personal outburst from the executant, the concept of an audience—a receiving mechanism—has to be reckoned with : and an audience is more than the sum of its parts, and it has to be got at partly through the *creation* of a theatrical aura. This aura to-day cannot be devised out of the raw material that was suitable for dance-presentations at, say, Epidauros two thousand five hundred years ago.[6]

In a retrospect of the past forty years, the historic scene is thickly scattered with personalities offering different kinds of message or preaching philosophies through what they believed were exciting theatre methods. In the cases of all but an odd dozen or so, they were constantly betraying their misunderstanding of the function of the theatre in our time. The Americans, still considerably divided off from each other, have not invaded European theatres in sufficient density or frequency to make any marked impression either on their European counterparts or on the native dance-audiences which, to a surprising extent, are willing to be shown something new. On the other hand, it is precisely those Europeans who paused and took thought, then set to work *through* a theatrical organisation, who have won out, theatrically speaking. The best of them have created theatre styles of movement, of differing degrees of validity, which do make an impact on an audience not composed exclusively of friends and pupils. The highest degree of theatrical effectiveness is found in the system of Kurt Jooss, exactly because all its workings out have been made with an exact appreciation of the audience-performer relationship. A study of his works, and of the growth of his company and his school, shows that a continual line of progress is being maintained ; research still goes on, the teaching method grows more precise ; the dancer is called upon more and more to contribute the fruits of his personality to the shaping of the work in hand : the sympathy with ideas to be given expression, and the finding of the exact shade of dance-style to make that expression—all this is evidence that Jooss has not for a moment rested on his laurels. That he has created about thirty works of Ballet, in addition to directing a school, furnishing artistic direction, producing the works and dancing in them, all the time working out a system which is still growing and whose still unrealised potentialities must stem from his personal work, is proof that his achievement already equals that of any choreographer who has arisen to give fresh life to the art of Dancing and change its direction into pathways which are truly progressive.

III

· THE HISTORICAL NECESSITY OF JOOSS

THE creation of the dance method of Kurt Jooss and its application in the Theatre of our time forms, historically, the first phase of the biggest revolution that Ballet has yet undergone. Earlier than this, the outstanding reformist movements were those of Noverre and Fokine. Noverre's precepts were probably most successfully embodied in the works of Vigano, the last significant choreographer before the Romantic Age of Ballet. It could probably be shown that had Vigano's ballets been allowed to live into the Romantic period they might have channelled the Noverre teachings into the stream of tradition, and thus carried over his influence into the early nineteenth century. As it was, everything for which Noverre stood was swept away during the early period of the Romantic Ballet of Fillipo Taglioni, Perrot and Saint-Leon. The general call to order that Fokine issued in the form of a manifesto in 1904, was heard by most contemporary choreographers ; that revived consideration for proportion and a degree of æsthetic integration between Dance, Painting and Music (which is evident in most works created on the Diaghilev organisation up to 1929), is the fruit of his summarising of the art's most pressing needs at the start of his career.

The two movements of reform had, broadly, the same aim—to draw attention to a decadence which had occurred, at two periods one hundred and fifty years apart, from an excessive regard for tradition. Noverre saw through the inanities of convention which were strangling the French Ballet of his time. He not only injected some sense and order into the choreographic and teaching practices of the eighteenth century, but he also invented the " action ballet," a considerable step forward from the elaborate suite-de-danse type of work commonly in vogue before his time. His fiery, ruthless, and remarkably sensible collection of " Letters on the Art of Dance " was published in all the major European languages during his lifetime, and his influence was so strong that most of his reforms had been accepted before he achieved in old age his Mecca—the Paris Opera. Yet he was a man of the eighteenth century, and his lessons have to be relearned in every generation. The specific advice that Noverre has to offer is valuable only if it is referred to the social and artistic conditions within which the choreographer works. In this sense, perhaps, Noverre has placed his mark on all Ballet since his day by being spiritually available to all choreographers who have been unwilling to have their thinking done by others. So it might be argued that Fokine's stature as a reformer rests on his acceptance, after a century of undiluted Romanticism, of Noverre's dicta concerning artistic quality, unification of factors and the use of imagination.

During the process of restating Noverre's position in the history of Ballet, Fokine had taken over certain concepts which held good in Noverre's time, but which were scarcely strictly applicable to the early twentieth century. Noverre cared that Ballet should be a great and a noble art, but his references for Greatness and Nobility were the social conditions of his age. In so far as he was deferring to the eighteenth century's appreciation of the principle of Unity and a " classical " simplicity, he was doing no more than bringing the art into line with the advanced artistic and philosophical thought of the day. But the artist of to-day works with a quite different body of forms and materials than did his predecessor one hundred and fifty years ago. The changed constitution of European society has created fresh systems of ideas which influence the lives of all men living, to some degree. The great barriers that exist between our age and that of Noverre are the growth, since his period, of a dominantly urban and entirely mechanised milieu, and the creation of many grades of social differentiation. These have made a fresh sort of mental background for the artist ; for, all other things being equal, the artist to-day is as much the sum of his social conditioning as was his eighteenth century predecessor.

The vast multiplication of human beings since 1750, and the parallel multiplying of forms of employment, of cultural and social distinction, of standards of living, have changed the face of the world considerably : and, beyond even this amount of difference, we have to note the complexities which have grown into the texture of our civilisation because we have not only begotten the Machine, but we have apparently not yet learned how to thwart its efforts to master us. We cannot ignore the hard fact that we live inside a complex and very unstable form of society : by being a part of that society the artist is subject to its violence and instability, and this awareness of the world around him comes out in his work. Now, however much he may be the prophet, and the visionary whose gaze can penetrate the fogs of irrelevance which cling about the questions that all men seek to answer, the artist is also, and to a certain degree inescapably, a mirror of his times. His work, if not over-disciplined by too much deference to tradition, will show somewhere a crystallisation of those values which set a defined—if wavering—borderline between man and beast ; and which are the outcome of thousands of years of that struggle to which man has applied his unconquerable mind and his unbreakable heart. They are, in fact, the expression of god in man, and are the fibre which holds together the structure of all European myths, lore and philosophies. *The symbolic restating of these values is the formal justification for any work of art, and by the intensity of these restatements we are kept aware of the fundamental unity of all mankind.* It is this quality which defines the narrowness or width of the range of appeal to the largest number of different sorts of people : and this, in the last analysis, is the measure of the greatness of all choreographic creation. By his awareness of confusion in the world, the artist by-passes confusion in his work, and comments on great issues simply and movingly : but this is only possible to the artist who has completely accepted the age in which he lives, who does not incline wishfully to an age which is gone, and whose work is, therefore—and inescapably—concerned chiefly with Content and only secondarily with Form. From these considerations the fundamental artistic weakness in the traditional form of Ballet, as practised in the twentieth century, can be deduced.

That weakness was the inability of the people inside Ballet to see that because their art was the most highly formalised, the theatrical art most completely removed from the actuality of the world outside the theatre, it was the one least capable of absorbing, digesting, and presenting afresh the sort of ideas that dominate the social (and therefore the cultural) life of Europe to-day. In fact its particular stylisation was based on a visual æsthetic ; whatever the dancer's body was doing, it was all the time giving a consciously devised expression to the notion of a certain sort of physical beauty. All Ballet is conditioned by this factor. It is a *seen* art primarily, and an expressive one (in terms of ideas, intellectual concepts of any sort) only secondarily. The idea-basis fixed in the eighteenth century had held good throughout the nineteenth, and the social conditions against which the main academic and producing system (the Russian) was being developed, strengthened this ideological concept. To any choreographer prior to Fokine, Ballet was an art giving expression, through dance-and-mime formulas, to the notion of the social desirability of nobility, grandeur and remoteness.

Noverre's protests had been right, for his time; so were Fokine's for his. But Fokine failed to appreciate that a hundred and fifty years had gone by, and, amongst other things that had changed, was the belief that nobility, grandeur and remoteness constitute the important social virtues. He calculated, accurately, that there was still a place for a highly stylised art such as Ballet in contemporary Europe, but what he apparently failed to realise was that its high degree of stylisation was just what prevented it from being the fully expressive form of theatrical dancing that the cultural trend of the century would certainly demand. (This realisation, later on in life, may account for his excessive contempt for all forms of Modern Dance.)

There is little evidence warranting the assumption that the traditional form can expand theatrically much further. Technically, as to Dance, Acting, Decor, Costume, Music, Stagecraft, almost everything that can be devised has been done since 1919. Since Fokine, the choreographers Massine, Nijinska, Balanchine and Tudor have by their respective manipulations of the plastic, technical, musical and intellectual elements of the classic dance (and its ancillary crafts), pushed the form through all the calculable mutations that its theatrical formulas will permit. All their work, Massine's new field of plastic potential, Nijinska's range of new precisions in dance execution, Balanchine's musical sub-

tleties and Tudor's skill in superimposing the subconscious on the conscious in his characters' behaviour patterns ; all is theatrically dependent for success on an absolutely visual æstheticism. The works of these creators emphasise the very specialised quality that a heavily stylised art must manifest. Because no other art-form approximates to its stylistic rigour of technique, and the delicacy of its proportionate structure (the balance to be achieved between the differing emotional pressures of Music, Painting and Dancing), it is an art whose total beauties are only appreciable by those conditioned to it : which makes it without doubt the most refined of all the contemporary arts—so refined that it is almost entirely without contact with the extra-theatrical world of to-day. No ballet in the traditional form, for instance, dealing with any social, moral or philosophical issue can say as much or as pointedly to any arbitrarily selected group of people (such as constitutes an audience) as a pamphlet, poem, song, film or play on the same subject. The channel of communication is too narrow.

This remoteness from actuality has been accepted as a condition of ballet-making ; yet, because the major arts of Poetry, Music, Drama and Painting have in this century become adjusted ideologically to the times, it seems likely that such specialised theatrical arts as Opera and Ballet will survive our epoch only if they accept as wide a field of cultural reference as do these other arts. This can come about through the acceptance of a wider fund of ideas for expressive purposes ; Kurt Jooss's impact on the theatrical dance is seen to be measurable in terms of the expressionism that his art can give to ideas growing from contemporary man's preoccupation with the contemporary world.

Our world contains all the glory and all the wreckage of the past : and in it lie the seeds of the future. Man's chief interest is, still, Man ; and this interest can be stimulated and rewarded by the arts in proportion to their ability to shed light on his problems, teach him philosophic lessons and direct his moral leanings. These processes need not be devoid of beauty ; the dance method of Jooss substitutes a different æsthetic, but it is one compounded of other elements than the purely visual. The method of physical expressiveness used in the New Dance is regulated by laws which existed (whether formulated or not) when the earliest dancers moved in front of the first audiences. The work that Laban and Jooss undertook seeks to codify those laws and to show their applicability to every problem of movement and gesture that can occur in the Theatre. And this is the measure of the importance of the New Dance to the twentieth century European Theatre.

The traditional method and the New Dance method are both theatrically successful : in the one case everything is filtered through the *personal* expressive potential of any given dancer in any part. (As audiences a hundred years ago went to see, not " Giselle," but Carlotta Grisi in " Giselle," so to-day the chief attraction of Ballet is the display of personality by the dancers.) In the case of the New Dance the intention is otherwise, it is to give the *dramatic* elements of the composition the primary emphasis. Kurt Jooss's approach to theatrical dance may be defined in these words (a free paraphrase of various of his published and private writings) : " The medium of the dance is the living human body with the power to convey ideas inherent in its movements. In what may be called pure or absolute dance, ideas of movement develop as they spring from the plastic imagination of the choreographer—an imagination which works with movement, shape and form. These ideas by their combination, their rise and fall, their contrasts, harmonies and conflicts, weave the pattern of dance which translates the spectator into a sphere of imagination where experiences of a particular vitality and beauty await him. In the dramatic dance, on the other hand, these pure imaginings of movement are fused with the dramatic idea, and the fusion of the two elements creates a new entity, the dance drama, whose subject-matter is the thought of the creator crystallised into active and suffering human characters. Its medium and its language is the dance, sequences of movements which have been subjected to the process of composition, which have been purified and harmonised in regard to each other, and in their relation to the space and rhythm which they create. This

to what we call gracefulness of the body in the movements : the intention is to life in their everchanging interplay ; To reflect these forces requires a ment—the dancer's body. The pro- the body consists in first experiencing in body, mind and soul, then in exter- all that is happening within us."

new art of Dancing is not confined and general beauty of line and rhythm give an image of the various forces of that is, a manifestation of Nature. purified and polished reflecting instru- cess of reflecting these forces through and studying them within ourselves nalising by corresponding movements,

In contrast to the traditional method exact shade of inflection, the precise degree of time and space co-ordination, Jooss the act of choreographic creation The dancer's body, considerably assisted a reflecting instrument. This does not Jooss ballet goes on stage with a sug- and then creates spontaneously on the does mean that while the ballet is in a conscious and co-operating partner in wishes to express is discussed with the

of composing dance, whereby the detail of movement and the absolute are set by the choreographer, with Kurt is a much more co-operative process. by the dancer's mind, is to be used as mean, of course, that the dancer in a gested plot or atmosphere in mind, groundwork of that theme. But it process of composition, the dancer is that process. What the choreographer dancer, because in this method what

is given expression is rather more important than how it is expressed. This seems a less diffuse and undisciplined affair when one recalls that the subject-matter is the *raison d'etre* for the ballet ; and that subject-matter is the expression of certain processes of thought fit for theatrical projection.

The general characteristic differences between Traditional Ballet and the New Dance : the traditional form gives expression primarily to visual concepts of grace, control, fluidity, speed, balance, through a technique of refined difficulty. The dancer is an interpretive mechanism for the choreographer's thought. The method is based on custom rather than law (the technique being derived from conceptions of bodily relationships first adumbrated three hundred years ago). Trial-and-error methods have been the means of extending the technique, and distinctive personal style is what, finally, places one dancer higher than another in the appreciator's catalogue. The basic rule for traditional Ballet is that What is done is less important than How it is done. . . . Jooss's dance method grows out of a refusal to accept this traditional method as the perfect form of theatre-dance expression. Few of the older form's technical usages are incorporated in his system, which has been created outward from a formulation of certain laws, which, he suggests, were probably once known but have fallen into disuse, and have actually vanished altogether from the canon of the traditional system. His contention is that the classical dance training sets the dancers' bodies in certain habits, some groups of muscles will only co-ordinate with given other groups. He begins by training the body to that degree of relaxation wherein the dancer can activate any part of it independently of any other part. Even the highly stylised movement of theatrical dancing should grow from a mental and nerve co-ordination of prompting to the muscles, *i.e.*, the dancer should not be able to make a movement completely automatically. The activation of his body flows from his mental awareness of the sort of movement it *should* be making, and (perhaps a long way back and almost sub-consciously) he is aware of the reason why it should be that specific movement. At this point it would be desirable to examine the technical premises from which Jooss laboured to create a system which would make possible the birth of a

theatrical dance supporting a different æsthetic from that of the traditional Ballet.

Jooss had danced as a child, for his own pleasure, and presumably that of his family, but had not thereby been committed to a dancing career. He was of an age when he could take decisions with some awareness of their importance, when he first began work in the Theatre. His approach was through Music, and it is possible that this detachment from the actual physical business of dancing was of the greatest help in allowing him to undertake the objective examination of theatrical dance which began with his first contact with Laban. How much of the new choreographic method, or of the technical system which supports it, is due absolutely to either one or the other, would be difficult to assess. Both worked in such close sympathy, such harmonious accord, during the time that Jooss was absorbing the enormous conception of the space laws of movement revealed by Laban. We may take it that Laban was the philosopher and researcher who first formulated the new conception of movement, and Jooss was the person with theatrical ability who could systematise it into an effective method. Laban had many other outstanding pupils and collaborators, but none of them had so completely absorbed all the investigations of the great teacher, elaborated them into a new style of movement and metamorphosed them into a dance method having dramatic expressiveness and theatrical suitability, as Kurt Jooss has done.

Laban's point of departure seems, most obviously, to have been the Platonic view of the Cosmos, for, from mathematical and scientific hypotheses advanced in Plato's work (notably " The Timæus ") is developed his enquiry into the nature and purpose of bodily movement, and the mental and neural impulses which guide and shape it. At what point the investigations first grew into a methodology is not certain. Laban himself made experimental dances and ballets on the student-colleagues (including Jooss) who worked with him in Hamburg in the early 'twenties, whilst Jooss was also making dances, gymnastic experiments, studying movement and gesture at every source he could reach. These early works by both are now lost, and are to be regarded as trial workings-out of, perhaps, some notion discovered in Delsarte, or a fresh muscular or rhythmic problem. All the technical developments which had come to the European Theatre in recent years were discussed and analysed by Laban and Jooss in their search for any precedent which might help towards the clarifying of their task. To give to theatrical dance a simple significance which could make it comprehensible and immediately meaningful—to make it truly expressive—it was necessary first to discard every article of belief attached to the traditional form. The two key names which point to the principal sources of material ultimately used by Jooss, are Plato and Delsarte.

The body is a co-ordinated whole (or rather, can be trained to be so : we have lost the faculty of spontaneous co-ordination somewhere on the road from Eden). Different parts of its complicated mechanism perform different functions, but the whole body can obviously give most meaningful expression when used wholly. When the art of Dance becomes theatrically effective through the manipulation of the whole body all the time, and not through systems which train the legs, the arms, the head, the torso, for different sorts of expressionism, it is obvious that the human anatomy can be made to " speak " a universal tongue. Five centuries of traditional development had shut theatrical dancing off from any idea of using the whole body all the time. Laban's basic work was to investigate the potential of the body in an attempt to rediscover, and, if possible, formulate,

the laws of its action, so that a New Dance method could arise independent of, and to some degree complementary to, the rigorously disciplined classical method. The investigations covered an analysis of Platonic teaching, for, Laban felt, certain of Plato's observations on proportional interrelations between all forms of life, should offer a clue to the discovery of the basic laws of bodily movement.

In a sense all scientific thinking inherited by our civilisation begins with the first Greek thinkers. All attempts to correlate Cause and Effect, enquiries into the nature of matter, the order of the cosmos and the structural principles behind all organic life were recorded in documents which to-day are remarkable for the conclusions reached by men working in small groups and with practically no kind of scientific apparatus. Pythagoras was the great genius of mathematics, and his enquiry into the nature of numbers and geometry provided a method which was applied by a later thinker and teacher, Plato, to the definition of the nature of the cosmic order and its parts. Plato's great documentaries, and particularly " The Timæus," are fascinating because of the existence in them of truths which have not yet been completely adapted into our thought and our implements of culture. From Plato we get the notion of a limited number of " shapes " which he thought must be the shapes of the units comprising the elements of Earth, Fire, Air and Water. It is significant that twentieth century mathematical and crystallographic research, with their successive penetrations into the structure of the atom and the crystal, reveal that Plato's teaching was based on a con-

siderable degree of truth, arrived at both by deductive and intuitive processes. The fundamental shape which occurs in every form of inorganic life is the triangle. Since the beginning of civilisation the triangle has dominated, inspired and conditioned every concept in which the notion of proportion was manifest. The awareness that some theory of proportion and a theory of space relations existed at the back of all structure—mathematics, architecture, music, to name three of the earliest sciences—had been in men's minds from the beginning. The theory of space-relations

might also, considered Laban, be applicable to the human anatomy. The tensions to which all parts of the body could be subjected, in relation to the maximum amount of air-space the body could occupy, seemed likely to be a fixed quantity defined by proportional relations. Some investigations and trial-and-error exercises and computations showed that this was so. The space-element, the regularised mathematical shape that absolutely expresses the harmonious correlation existing between all the possible movements of head, limbs and torso, is the icosahedron. This figure is one of Plato's four regular solids ; and is the amount of space contained within twenty equilateral triangles which are formed by the assembly of thirty equal sides. In the space lying within these boundaries exists a system of relations and stresses (between the dimensions of height, width and length, and the four maximum diagonal lines) corresponding to the tensions, oppositions and equilibria that the body in natural development can compass.

How far this knowledge, of the primary relationship between the organic thing which is a body, and the inorganic expression which is one of Plato's " regular shapes," can be extended is incalculable. It is a starting point for enquiry into that field where organic and inorganic meet. The most up-to-date mathematical and crystallographic research does not yet supply answers to all the questions arising from the discovery of this fixed law of proportion in human movement. The discovery of the existence of this organic-cum-inorganic spatial concept reveals that there is a completely new apparatus as a basis for philosophic and psychologic speculation. When we reflect on the

32

incidence, both as absolute shape and as concept, of triangle, tetrahedron, cube, circle, with the refinements of spiral and ellipse, in everything that Man has devised by his brain or wrought with his hands (everything—from the building of the Pyramids to the Dnieper Dam : from the hewing of the Cretan labyrinth to the shaping of an aircraft fuselage) we realise just how little we yet know of the subtleties of inter-relation between Man and the other components of Living.[7]

This formulation of movement-laws for the body formed, as it were, one half of the technical raw material to Jooss's hand : the other half was the expression code devised a hundred years ago by François Delsarte. Delsarte should be a great name in the European Theatre, yet apart from Wolkonsky's introduction of his teachings to the Petersburg Academy about 1910 and in Paris about 1928, one recalls few instances of his pedagogy occurring in the tradition of classical dance.[8]

Delsarte was French, born 1811, and was an abandoned orphan living in the streets of Paris at the age of 10. He had a natural passion for singing, and to fix the music of songs he learned from beggars and market-women, he invented a system of notation which he marked out on the sands of the Tuileries Gardens. He was found so occupying himself one day by a music teacher, who protected him and got him a place in the Conservatoire. Owing to the inconsistent manner in which his Conservatoire training had been applied, his voice completely failed at the age of 23, and he devoted the rest of his life to teaching and devising a system of gesture and expression for singers. Actually he did not devise ; his studies were the practical result of research, not only through all the literature of Rhetoric, but in the sphere of comparative anatomy in hospitals and mortuaries. There is a certain literature on the Delsartean method, most of it published in the last century : the principal disciple was Genevieve Stebbins, who has ordered the material into documents which, with their detailed pictorial diagrams, give full exposition to this universal system of " correspondences." The best précis existing on Delsarte is found in Lincoln Kirstein's " Ballet Alphabet " (Kamin Publishers, New York, 1939) under the sectional heading " Gesture," and the following quotations are from that work. " Students of the dance often despair that gesture cannot be learned in an academy like the classic ballet. There is a considerable literature on the subject, both ancient and modern, from Cicero and Quintilian to Sir Charles Bell, the anatomist, and Mantegazza, the criminologist. However, for those seriously interested in practical results rather than historical curiosities, almost everything of value may be limited to studies attributed to François Delsarte. This remarkable man, who published nothing while alive, left sufficient material to provide a fundamental background for a universal academy of gesture. Famous as a teacher during his life, he enjoyed an even more remarkable posthumous reputation, particularly in America, from 1880 to 1900. However, lacking his presence to activate his theories, his system, as promulgated by his heirs, fell under the severe and just criticism of being purely mechanical and arbitrary. The apostolic fervour of his disciples may easily have been fanatic, but this does not excuse the disfavour and ridicule which has subsequently obscured his essentially important contribution. . . . To be sure, a few contemporary dramatic teachers employ his underlying structure of expression, but its large system, which is, in fact, an analysis and ordering of all effective gesture, is ignored or unknown by those very students of dancing who, in search of a basic skeleton for pantomime, might need it most. Delsarte claimed no particular originality for his studies. They were the practical results of research, not only through the classic rhetoricians, but of comparative anatomy in clinics, morgues and hospitals. His reluctance to publish is perhaps significant. His contact was directly with his pupils. His generalisations were for their use, not as arbitrary formulæ for mechanical application, but as a kind of plastic geometry for universal correspondence. Delsarte did for gesture and, indirectly, for dancing, what the other great formulators of the nineteenth century accomplished for their chosen fields. As Comte in exact science, Ruskin in æsthetics, Buckle, J. S. Mill, or even Marx, in historical analysis, and Carlo Blasis in the classic theatrical dance, so Delsarte provided an apparatus for the investigation and use of gesture." . . . The system is founded on a sub-dividing of the human organism into relations-of-three (the triangularity occurring again, as in the icosahedral concept outlined above). Man is to be thought of in a triune state—emotional, intellectual and sensitive (or physical). The body is considered in three separate divisions, the head representing the intellectual nature, the limbs the physical, and the torso the emotional. These again are divided into trinities; and though this sub-dividing extends down to defining the intellectualism of the foot, for instance, the important thing about the whole system is the way in which the co-ordinations between parts of the anatomy reveal a practically unlimited corpus of gesture and pantomimic play, in which the whole, *or any part*, of the body can be significantly used. Over this formulation of the trinities, and trinities of trinities, Delsarte elaborates nine laws of gesture, and for much of the psycho-physiological propriety of these he is indebted to Charles Darwin's documentary on emotional expression in men and animals. He enunciates a series of " breaking down " exercises to give every part of the body relaxation and utterly free movement; from this " broken down " condition of the anatomy, which is really a separating for gestural purposes of each part of the body, the dancer builds up any gesture by a process of composition.

The appreciation by Jooss of how much might be wrought out of these technical precepts—of the spatial conditioning of the body by Plato's suggested laws, and of a wholly scientific vocabulary of gesture—was aided rather than limited by his study of the formal basis of the classic dance. For much of the training idiom of the classic dance is used in the classes given to the Jooss dancers. He has never, as so many other innovators have done, derided the Classical Ballet method, but he has seen its limitations as well as been aware of its beauties. From its methodology he has taken certain elements which help in training his dancers to the requisite degree of plasticity, and some others which he can legitimately use for expressive purposes. Yet there are observably few strictly Classical steps or technical feats (such as the double air turn, the sustained repetitive pirouette) embodied in his system. The quality cannot be termed less than genius which is displayed in the welding together of these various components to make a dance idiom as completely theatrically effective (though in different terms) as the Classical Ballet method. This successful development of the Form has only come about because all the time there has been a large incentive; that incentive has been from the first, and is still to-day, to make the dancer's body reflective of those impulses, whether emotional, spiritual or intellectual, which are the gamut of all human behaviour.

IV

THE BALLETS OF KURT JOOSS

THE differences, both of intention and of method, between the traditional and the Jooss systems, do not exist as two irreconcilable answers to the same question, or as two insoluble problems. These differences grow from opposing viewpoints concerning the aim of theatrical dancing : whilst the new method is intrinsically opposed to most of the ideologies and practices of the traditional form, it is not claimed to be, in itself, the most complete, or the final, method of theatrical dance creation. Jooss does claim that his style of choreography—which works through a different method towards an essentially dramatic end—is as proper to the Theatre as that older system which allows dramatic considerations to be secondary to visual satisfaction.

The history of Ballet shows us that the method derived from and through Beauchamps, Noverre, Vigano, Blasis, does not fulfil all the theatrical requirements which could be expected from a Theatre of the Dance. European dramatic art is descended from a form which was, originally, a drama of mime and music. Mime, at its fullest early development was capable of producing fully theatrical effects upon an audience. The absolute essence of Drama is Mime. Ballets in which the drama takes precedence over the atmospheric or lyrical components are essential to a living Theatre of Dancing.

The fact that actors, in any sort of dramatic happening, require production to make all their effectiveness fully theatrical, points to the essentially stylistic nature of all dramatic art : and the essence of production (the sum of all the external factors working upon and around the actor to give him the best usage of his personal instrument—the voice) is movement. That movement is, inevitably, stylised movement, the true basis therefore not only of dance but of acting. That which gives final and full significance to every performer in the Theatre is movement. The application of this basic truth to a consideration of both dramatic material and technical dance-forms is what lies behind the Jooss ballets. From the traditional system he has taken certain movements, and the analysis of the neuro-muscular basis of those movements has justified his using them in his method of dance composition. His avoidance of some of the obviously attractive parts of the older technique is not a lack of appreciation of their potentialities, but an unwillingness to make more than a minimum of compromise. Because the conditions for ballet-making from the mid-seventeenth century to 1900 emphasised the qualities of physical superiority, remoteness and non-reality (which form a gloss

35

on the surface of the tough muscularity of its technique) it is a less suitable method for creating dramatic dance than the Jooss method. From these considerations it is apparent that Jooss's major contention stands up to examination and dissection. That contention, which is implicit in every dance or ballet that he has ever made, is that the traditional form of Ballet cannot compass everything that may be expressible in the Voiceless Theatre, whereas the Jooss form of Ballet does give theatrical expression to certain concepts beyond the reach of the older method. They are thus complementary to one another—certainly so at this stage in the history of post-Noverre Ballet when Fokine's renaissance has burned away to ashes and too few innovators on a scale comparable with Fokine have been evolved through the traditional system.

Since the beginning of his career Kurt Jooss has made about thirty ballets, of which one half have formed the repertoire of the Ballets Jooss since 1932; the others, from " A Persian Ballet," of 1924, to " Pulcinella," of 1932, which immediately preceded " The Green Table," were works made during the period of development. They show the result of all his considerations of how the new method could be shaped and directed so that the differing dramatic ideas behind " Tragödie," " Kaschemme," " Larven," " Room 13," etc., were given expression : they were steps taken during the building up of the style which is first fully revealed in " The Big City " and " The Green Table." This new concept of theatrical dance has made itself felt through the works of one man. (The exceptions in the total repertoire are Sigurd Leeder's ballet, " Sailor's Fancy " (1943), and a work by Agnes de Mille, " Drums Sound in Hackensack," created and danced only in America during 1940-42, when Jooss was absent from the company, and a first work by Hans Zullig, " Le Bosquet " (1945).) The Ballets Jooss, dancing in Jooss ballets since 1932, has by the hard fact of continuing to exist in the commercial Theatre justified the creation of this new style of Ballet ; the accolade of public, as well as of critical, appreciation has kept them alive. By now " The Big City " and " The Green Table " must have been danced well over two thousand times each, a distinction which probably only half-a-dozen ballets by Fokine and Massine can share during the past twenty years.

This consideration—of the absolute newness, the lack of any precedent in all the work that Jooss undertook—must govern all assessments of his works and their value. Few other choreographers can show an equivalent number of lasting ballets in the same period : during the fifteen years between his first work and the outbreak of war he built up a dance method, a school, a corps of teachers, a company of dancers and a repertory of works. For the first ten years, at least, he had full responsibility as choreographer, producer and artistic director of a Ballet organisation which played over the whole of Europe and North America.

The full list of works presented since the company's first visit to London includes all the larger ballets, together with all the surviving short ballets from the pre-1932 period : excluding the ballets by Leeder, de Mille and Zullig the catalogue is : " The Big City," " The Green Table," " A Ball in Old Vienna," " Ballade," " The Mirror," " Pavane," " Johann Strauss, To-night! " " The Prodigal Son," " The Seven Heroes," " Chronica," " A Spring Tale," " Company at the Manor " and " Pandora." Four works, in date order : " The Green Table," " The Mirror," " Chronica " and " Pandora " show four progressive phases in the crystallisation of their creator's thought and imagining as applied to certain major problems of human relationships which exist to harass artists no less than politicians and philosophers. These inescapable issues, which are in some degree personal problems also for every citizen of the contemporary world, might be defined in terms which would stand as sub-titles to the ballets listed above, viz. : The Realistic View of War, War in Retrospect, The Corruption of Power, The Necessity for Understanding.

In a unique way these four works present for our contemplation a

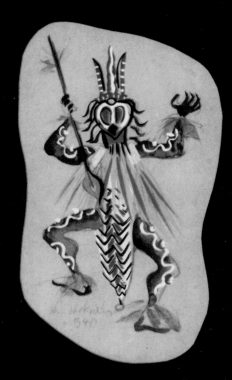 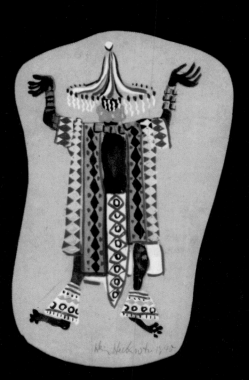

completely focused and perspectively accurate picture of the four inescapable political problems which, whether we approve or no, intrude upon our lives and influence our behaviour every day. They are not sermons, nor political tracts, they are works engaging our whole attention by the most legitimate of theatrical means—the assault upon the emotions and the reacting stimulation of thought, at a later instant of time.

"The Green Table" has been described as a present-day version of the Danse Macabre, as a satire on the League of Nations, as "red propaganda," and as several other curious things. From certain points of view, it may be each of these things to different people, but, in sum, it is a work covering much larger questions than these and with a wider reference than these particular matters imply. It is a non-romantic, and therefore, to a high degree realistic, picture of many aspects of warfare and its related social disturbances. Since the entire span of the twentieth century up to now has seen the whole of Europe intensely preoccupied with and, in large part, heavily engaged in warfare on a scale not hitherto imaginable, this ballet has an inescapable topicality which is to-day as pungent and disturbing as it was when the work was first seen in Paris in 1932.

"The Mirror" is in a sense a necessary sequel to "The Green Table," though, as a piece of theatrical expression, quite comprehensible to anyone unfamiliar with the earlier work. It poses a problem which in differing degrees of intensity has been agitating large numbers of suffering people in Europe practically continuously for centuries : the problem is that of the unbalance and frustrations engendered in those whose lives have been torn up by warfare, and who usually have to do violence to their own personalities in the process of re-adjusting themselves, after an experience for which nothing had prepared or forewarned them. The behaviour of several differing types during their efforts to attain a just psychological balance, is the theme of this ballet. Ten years ago this problem had a savage topicality, for only at that distance after the 1914-18 war was it being realised that this question of the maladjustment of whole sections of society to post-war social conditions was one of the primary reasons for so much social unrest, in whatever forms that unrest appeared. But just at this period (1935) there was growing a preoccupation with, and a dread of, another impending catastrophe. The deepening political corruption spreading over the whole of European society evolved a sort of natural conditioning to and a suitable background for the first totalitarian acts of aggression. The fast-moving tempo of political disorders tended to reduce such problems as those posed in "The Green Table" and "The Mirror" to a smaller perspective, and subsequently to cloud them over with the swift-gathering shadows of 1937, 1938 and 1939.

"Chronica" was in preparation throughout 1937 and 1938, and was first produced early in 1939 at a time when few voices of weight were heard protesting against gangster-politicos who, in the names of Christianity and Progress, had played in Africa and Spain respectively the prelude and opening aria of the tragedy which reached its climax in September of that year. Its scenario is of events in a mediæval city-state, in which is related the story of how a town

suffered under a powerful personality who was strong enough to create a dictatorship, and whose evil only began to be wiped out at his death. The highly dramatic narrative, involving feasts, dances, parliaments, battles, was strengthened by the full-sized humanity of the characters, both strong and weak, who developed the exciting story into one of the Theatre's more telling satires on dictatorship. Within six months the outbreak of war was bringing about that train of events which isolated the Ballets Jooss in America for over two years, and caused, among other things, the temporary abandonment of this work from the repertory. It has not been seen in this country since late 1939 ; when it is revived its satirically pointed moral lesson is likely to be still topical. At the same time a revival of "The Mirror" would have an even more pungent topicality, and in a world which will again learn the hard

way that primrose paths scarcely ever lead anywhere satisfactory, these works will automatically be accorded a high place in the avant-garde Theatre.

The wider canvas, embracing indirectly as parts of its macrocosmic subject-matter the content of these three earlier large-scale works, is seen in the ballet "Pandora," Jooss's first serious wartime creation, made after he had been unavoidably separated from his colleagues for three years. In this work the fundamental problem which lies at the back of all theorising and moralising about human behaviour is considered. It is the questioning of Man's ability—or even inclination—to attempt to make a working proposition of society; to refrain from creating the sort of inevitable evils which grow out of power-seeking, the unthinking satiation of appetites and unrestrained ambitiousness. And, deeper than these considerations, arises the question of his willingness and ability to abide by the eternal truths of Love and Peace. These are the matters which lie immediately under the surface of the skilful analogy and symbolism in which this work is clothed.

No ballet is precisely describable; words however carefully chosen, when used to describe things, will conjure up slightly variable images for several different people. They can give a recital of plot and action, and can convey certain impressions of the characterisations unfolded by the narrative; they can reveal the structure of the various dance-incidents and can suggest a part of what has been revealed of human behaviour, but in the last analysis, the seeing is all. What words can record are the most emphatic impressions made on the spectator; never the entire texture of the varying rhythms of Space and Time and Movement and Music which are the "nerve, bone and sinew" of theatrical dancing. The words can only have significance for someone who has already seen, or will at some time in the future see, the same ballets with a keen eye, an attentive ear and an open heart. Dance is the refined essence of the prime element in the Theatre, and the raw material of Dance is human bodies. An audience has an intrinsic power of assimilation of patterns of movement which, of themselves, make sense or create their own rightness. This fact is more important than that some component of the dance-style, whether æsthetic, inspirational or intellectual, be impressed upon the audience. The first requisite in a theatrical happening is the projection of dramatic action, and the ballets of Kurt Jooss fulfil this condition; they are as full of drama as an egg is of meat.

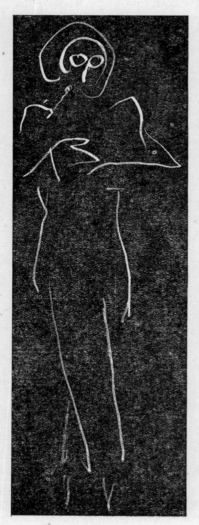

"The Big City" (1932) tells a straightforward dramatic story, and makes it the more poignant by outlining so clearly the hard realities in the lives of most town-dwellers in this age and civilisation. Since all the major European cities have attained the same degree of standardisation for their patterns of leisure, the to-and-fro evening promenade along Piccadilly, or the Boulevard St. Denis, the Kurfurstendamm, or Via Viente Settembre, is in each case comprised of the same elements. We see typists and clerks, the newsboy and prostitutes, factory girls and working lads; elegant and would-be-elegant men of leisure, a few tramps and fanatics, a sprinkling of touts, beggars and street-vendors walk, loiter, amble or trot briskly along. It is the evening cross-section of Main Street anywhere, made up almost entirely of those whose lives are too formless, or whose pockets are too light, to enjoy solitude and quiet leisure. The ballet's synopsis reads: "In the hurrying throng of a continental city are seen the Young Girl and the Young Workman, her sweetheart, homeward bound after the day's work. . . . The Libertine, in search of new conquests, follows the Young Girl to her home. . . . Dazzled by the promise of adventure she fares forth on his arm to the dance halls, where disillusion awaits her. . . ." In the opening scene, amidst the traffic of the city streets, the Young Man seeks the Girl, finds her amongst the pressing throng, and after the crowd has melted away they dance tenderly together. He dances his love for her, and his belief in her, and the moving softness and ease of their dance underlines their innocence, their simplicity and their need of each other. The Libertine appears in search of prey, and by his skilful insinuations he succeeds in making a violent impression on the naïve girl so that, dazzled by his charm, his wittiness and his promises, she can forget her lover and runs off enchanted on the arm of her new admirer. The Young Man, struck with rage and misery at such desertion, is left a helpless spectator of the abduction. Half of himself is torn away by this dreadful act, and he stands crushed with bitterness, bewildered, and in pain staring after them as they set off for their night's adventure. The second scene shows a poor neighbourhood where ragged, barefoot brats play happily, for awhile forgetful of their hunger. Into this scene runs the Young Girl, who is neighbour, perhaps even sister, of some of them; and with much ostentation the Libertine presents her with a box containing a gift. In a glow of gratitude and embarrassment she runs into her

home, leaving the Libertine nonchalantly idling as he waits her return. The brats have ceased their games, and with wondering eyes have seen the expensive gift change hands, they watch with curiosity this elegant stranger and then, sensing his inappropriateness in their dingy alley, they back away from him and their interest turns to hostility. Their mothers come outdoors to watch this strange adventurer and their neighbour's daughter; she returns, clad in evening finery of a kind evidently beyond her poor purse, and we know that this was the expensive gift of the Libertine. Swelling with conceit, he dances with the pretty, and by now adoring child, while the mothers of the street-urchins watch with grim understanding this first stage of the seduction he has undertaken. The children, now completely hostile, cower under the shelter of their mothers' arms as they all watch the cynical episode, and the Libertine, with exaggerated, courtly gestures leads the Young Girl away towards the bright lights. The mothers glare like thwarted tigresses, and the children, their courage returning, point mocking fingers after the couple as they dance away.

The scene moves to a dance-hall where stupid, doll-like youths and girls stamp and contort through the graceless motions of a debased kind of ballroom dance, and in their midst the Libertine and the Young Girl, intoxicated with excitement, dance with even wilder contortions than the rest. The music changes to a sadder, slower measure, and the ballroom figures glide away as their places are taken by a corresponding number of poor youths and their girls. Their dance is simple, easily rhythmical, and in the pattern of the dance each couple dreams itself away from the reality of the harsh working world for a time. The Youth enters seeking his lost love, and we know, as surely as he

42

knows, that already she is gone from him forever. He dances with one of the working girls, perhaps to try to regain for a few moments some of the ecstasy he knew before in this same dance-hall, or to relieve with violent action the strain of his fruitless and tiring search. Then the pattern of the sad and repetitive waltz closes in again, and he is left a lonely figure while the rhythm changes subtly back again to the earlier banal measure, and the first occupants of the hall are back again, among them the Sweetheart. The Youth presses through the crowd, both sorts of dancers weaving a complex pattern through which he pushes vainly trying to reach her. Then the groups change patterns, and the poor people glide away, the other dancers move altogether upstage ; the Youth is left quite alone, isolated from everyone as the lights dim slowly and he stands in a pool of soft light while the others fade into shadows. The lights dim more and more, the maddening stupid rhythm goes on and on, marked by the even stamp and shuffle of the dancing automatons who are happily ignorant and uncaring of the drama that is passing amongst them. The Youth, crushed with misery, stands alone staring blindly out into the night, still faintly visible at the downrush of the curtain.

In this work, which so keenly emphasises Drama rather than the beauties of Dance, Jooss has given a species of pictorial diagram of living in the modern industrial city. Its closest parallels in another form are the films " Rien que les heures " (Cavalcanti, 1926) and " Berlin : Symphony of a City " (Ruttmann, 1927).[9] But Jooss in his ballet is able to emphasise the separate components of the social texture in ways that these fine documentary films could not. The ballet assumes a tragic quality because the Simple Young Man realises the scale of his misfortune and struggles against it with inadequate weapons, doomed in advance to defeat.

The theatrical impressiveness of the work grows out of that reality which the characters possess when first we see them, and which they continue to sustain because their subsequent actions have psychologic truth. Inside twenty minutes' action there is etched with fine economy of line the design of the social pattern of the Machine Age city : the life of the Poor and the Bourgeois, the sad and sordid amusements of those who have, and the greyness of the lives of those who have not. It is at the same time an unstressed comment, for instance, on the difference between having and lacking ; on the uncertainty of the foundations upon which love rests ; and on the disquieting ways in which many of us behave when indulging consciously in a good time.

Apart from the cinematic cross-sectioning of the early documentaries, similar material has found its way into other forms of the Theatre. This cutting across a slice of life is the theme of Massine's " Jardin Publique," with its recital of a day's happenings in a city park. His sort of composition required a stylising not only of Dance, but also of Mime, of Decor, of Costume, carried to such intensity that the characters never had (were never intended to have) a semblance of flesh-and-blood reality. The Suicide, the Chair Vendor, Poor Lovers, Rich Lovers, Nursemaids, etc., are given in two-dimensional shapes because their *physical* portrayal in dance-action matters more than their credibility as persons. In this way they conform to balletic type, being credible only within the visually fantastic milieu of the theatrical park, as devised by Lurçat or Halicka. (The work had two schemes of decor and dress in two successive seasons.)

In " The Big City " the real-life character, as observed by Kurt Jooss in thousands of examples, is stylised through his system of dance, motion and gesture, into a theatrically plausible character. This theatrical plausibility convinces because it is stylised with such clarity out of extra-theatrical behaviour—everyday action and gesture—that the symbolism registers in full effect on each spectator. This sort of choreography can be called purely theatrical—if theatrical quality may be defined as the significant exaggeration of customary and recognisable actions and attributes. At the same time this choreography is highly revelatory of the world outside the Theatre because it brings into close focus the living character who is the archetype of the theatrical creation.

So the main pattern of the ballet is made up, apart from the specific dance-patterns introduced in the dance hall sequences, of " steps " built on all the variations of human locomotion—prancing, shuffling, ambling, gliding, hesitant, bold, or furtive—and a style of freely rhythmic and unstressed dance which shows more elasticity but less elevation, little line but plenty of roundness, in comparison with the classical Ballet. The dance-hall patterns used by the two different groups are strong and meaningful stylisings of, on the one hand, a violent hip-jerking variant of the Charleston, and on the other, a waltz in the spirit of the " Bal Musette " which alternates the turning-circles with long, pantherine, gliding steps.

Because the freer pattern of action is so different from a ballet with *entrées*, *pas seuls*, mime passages and corps-de-ballet masses, its visual " shape " cannot be described in terms of mathematic, architectural or musical pattern ; we watch characters moving inside space, rather than against a background, dispensing significant action during every second. The main directions of movement, to some extent imposed by the extensive dance-hall scenes, are long cross-stage lines and full-stage circles, though the diagonals are freely used and small circles are opposed to, or built towards, large circular movements : then, they are used as contrast in the successive scenes of the children playing and the first dance-hall. A dozen hints of circle imagery occur throughout the work, and they are significant because the idea of repetition, which connects with protracted action inside a small space, is being pushed, gently, into our attention, not because it is a convenient way of maintaining the flow of the pattern, but because the repetitive quality of the cycle is the mark which stands upon every kind of human activity. Equally, the straight line becomes a dramatic contingency when we see the mothers pacing up and down, with the crouching children sheltering underneath their arms, as they watch with unwavering gaze the hated Libertine who has intruded upon their lives. When, within the pausing circle in the dance-hall, the Youth suddenly begins to dance alone, his swift and widespread jumping pattern ebbs and flows around a tight, swaying stance which exactly expresses his instability and misery being overcome by his desperate effort to move everywhere—swiftly, blindly, but at once—in search of his lost love.

In " The Big City " we see, as in every other Jooss ballet, that every part of the dramatic effect of the dancing is underlined by the individual stagecraft which is a part of the Jooss production method. The most obvious novel factor is the emphasis placed on costume rather than on decor : when the reasons for this are perceived, we realise to what extent normal stage resources and equipment have been worked upon, in thought and by experiment, to serve the ends of dramatic dancing. To draw a simple analogy : because the characters are created as three-dimensional persons, the devices of stagecraft are used to give, as closely as possible, the actuality of three dimensions to the dancing figures on the stage.

Traditional Ballet has developed a convention (none the less valid and effective for being, mostly, unobvious) that the ultimate thing making for pure dancing style is Line : and Line is best created and manipulated through stressing the frontal plane of the dancer. The audience is directed, unconsciously, of course, towards seeing the dancer as an outline, a flat shape, having length and breadth (or call it height and width) but not depth. This convention has helped to create, and has in turn been fed by, every technical development since the days of Beauchamps.

The subject-matter for Jooss's work required, as we have seen, a technical method which stressed dramatic movement, and which could not, therefore, accept the two-dimensional shape as sufficient. To emphasise the complete wholeness of the dancer the style of costume used in Jooss ballets differs from the usual balletic type. Decor and

dress for Ballet have, almost uninterruptedly since its history began, been distinct from other sorts of theatrical decoration for body and stage. At some points the history of Ballet development has meant the history of costume changes which have helped, and even paralleled, technical developments by making for clearer, easier execution, and, in due proportion, increased spectacularism. The painted setting has come to be more imaginatively useful to the choreographer as it has become more an imaginative, rather than a realistic, piece of designing. In the hands of some choreographers it has been consciously integrated into the work as one of the harmony-concepts for their pictures (either moving or still) of bodies in costumes against stylised pictorial backgrounds. For the work of Kurt Jooss these considerations did not apply; the costumes in his works have to accentuate symbolism rather than decorativeness, and are planned outside the convention ruling for ballets by, for instance, Fokine and Massine. In these sorts of ballets, the costumes must (or ought to) suggest both character and symbolism, reveal period and locality reference, and allow for a more rapid, more aerial, and more extended kind of movement than is found in Jooss's work; further, they should assist the body, in slow movement or in stasis, to form visually satisfactory Line.

The three-dimensional concept which is to be projected (again, unconsciously, upon the audience) in the ballets of Jooss is accentuated by the unusually fluid lighting used in his productions. This can happen because painted setting is dispensed with (in some ballets furnishings and hangings are used; when they occur they occupy little space out of the entire black surround which is used for all the ballets). The box of the stage space can be treated as a cubic unit of variable dimensions; its height, width and depth can be altered by filling and emptying different areas, spots, surfaces and levels with Light. Light here becomes a truly plastic factor, probably for the first time in stage history successfully so. It is used architecturally, to give depth or solidity, to mask or to reveal, to emphasise, by slow insistence or violent suddenness, the importance of the lone figure or the group. At any second in the action the space revealed is the dramatically necessary space for that point in the action; the shape and extent of the spaces being infinitely variable (inside the dimensions of that particular stage) and being altered by the volume, colour, and direction of flow of the Light used. This, a most strenuous task for director and stage staff at any performance, is as carefully planned as to timing, density and colour-tone as are the physical rhythms of the dance patterns or the music which accompanies them.

" The Green Table " is a story of war, and treats its subject with honesty, clarity, and a lack of romanticising which, far from stressing the sordid and the gruesome, underlines the real-life events from which the work is stylised and gives them a cathartic quality which shakes the heart, and at the same time, clears the mind. Outside the Theatre of spoken drama this is possibly the first time that war has been treated imaginatively, yet in an adult way, on the stage. Because it happened at a time when its comprehensive treatment of causes and effects in modern warfare coincided with a widespread interest in the notion of the undesirability of war, it has acquired the value of a classic of modern ballet. In some cases this fact has been directed into a pretence that this is Jooss's one serious and successful work: a performance of " The Prodigal Son," " Chronica " or " Pandora " will help any unbiassed spectator to correct this misapprehension. Not for a moment in this ballet is the glamorous aspect of warfare allowed to intrude, here is no flattering of those childhood impressions, culled from story-books, of war as a series of pictures of hand-to-hand fighting between handsome and muscular toughs in fancy dress. Instead, the very essence of the tragedy of warfare is revealed in the stressing of the amount of further misery let loose on the earth; a misery which has to be borne and gradually paid off by both the generation involved, and the succeeding generation.

It is already possible to interpret the movements of European history since 1860 as a partly-directed, partly-aimless flowing together of the moral, political and economic pressures which are found in the European system, towards the struggle for the final hegemony of the Western world. These pressures manifest themselves, ultimately, in war; and the series of minor European wars from 1860 onwards formed precedents, excuses and, in the end, justifications for this century's outbursts. Occurring within that dark period of human history, the twenty-one years stretching from 1918 to 1939, this ballet pointed back to the object lesson that 1914-18 should have been, and pointed forward to the possibility of a recurrence within our lifetimes.

By presenting a picture of what war really means in the heavily industrialised twentieth century, the work has a topicality for this first half of the century, and for as far forward as we can imagine into the latter half. The title refers to the conference table at which diplomats, statesmen and other arbiters of destiny foregather for the resolving of problems. Kurt Jooss has not been unwilling to suggest that men with enormous powers of decision are seldom inspired with a willingness to see and sympathise with the other man's point of view.

The action occurs in six scenes set between prologue and epilogue, which depict the incidents around the green table leading to, and growing out of a war. At the curtain's rise we see gathered at the table the ten negotiators clad in formal black and wearing grotesque masks; they suggest by means of these false-faces every sort of professional political type: here are the studious, the unworldly, the priestlike and the dreamer, the proconsul, the man-of-fashion and the intriguer.

46

Princess   Hein Heckroth '39

The Prince   Hein Heckroth '39

Hein Heckroth '39

Hein Heckroth '39

They spring to life at the rise of the curtain and begin their disputations as the guardians of nations, the planners of civilisations, the yes-men of international cartels. The right note has been already struck, the emphasis here is on the general unfitness of these men for the enormous responsibility they wield, for since the time of the Congress of Vienna there have been few occasions upon which international arbitration was carried out by men with any sense of true internationalism. They smile, persuade, flatter, argue, then rage at one another. They threaten and gesticulate wildly with harsh, puppet-like movements which stress the unreality of the emotions to which they pretend. They go through a formula of discussion; they understand, then they apologise, they resume their chattering until their mutual hatreds impel them to a mutual rage. At this point they leave the table, pacing up and down, back and forth, with the agitation of bantam-cocks or the wariness of foxes: the moment of tension passes and with even deeper bows and cruder flatteries they forgive each other and, moving towards the table, begin again the insincere platitudes, the exchanging of clichés, and the rest of the verbiage which forms the stock-in-trade of their depicted profession. . . . The tension rises again, and as they reach the point of absolute and unrelenting antagonism, they mask themselves in the dignity of intransigence and separate into ten uncompromising units. With one gesture they draw ten ridiculous pistols from their ten pockets and fire into the air ten simultaneous shots. This symbolic violence releases an ever-expanding pattern of violence in which perhaps ten times ten thousand will die, and ten times that number suffer lifelong injury, loss, or avoidable personal tragedy.

The action flows through six scenes depicting the assembling of the forces, their training, their journey to battle: we see the battlefield, the brothel, and the dark roads where wander the homeless and stricken refugees. We see courage and cowardice rendered useless; watch the extremities of futile slaughter. Men follow a bright banner which leads the way to death; bedraggled, it becomes a symbol of hope in the outcome of the final struggle. But the odds are, as ever, against the pawns and very early in the narrative we are aware that soldiers, wives, sweethearts, mothers, will lose all to at least one of the only two possible winners in this picture: the Profiteer and the Figure of Death. It is they that the odds favour; yet in the end even the Profiteer cannot circumvent or buy off the partner with whom he had at first gladly co-operated, and Death sweeps the ridiculous chess game off the board and scoops up pawns, knights, bishops, rooks, queens and kings. Throughout the action he is present, striking a chill into all hearts, sapping desire, corrupting ability, as he hovers in the background or stalks steadily, mechanically and undeviatingly through scenes of battle, flight, or surrender. Here is Death presented starkly, Death as mediæval man knew him, the figure of the " Danse Macabre," the grinning skeleton whose scythe will cut away all men's loves and hopes, fears and ambitions.

This drama presents in microcosm the realities of modern warfare, and the whole character list is compassed by not more than twenty dancers. Diplomats become soldiers, wives, mothers; the type figures are conveyed by seven or eight persons. The work is paralleled by a musical score of becoming simplicity and aptness, which lacks pretension and all other qualities of a purely virtuoso character. It is scored for two pianos and serves convincingly the primary

49

purpose of music in all Jooss ballets—to move alongside the dancing, alternating with it at times in conveying an atmospheric or lyrical note, but never dominating its shapes or movement rhythms. The dancing embraces the same range of real-life movement " signatures " as are found in " The Big City " with the addition of strong characterising patterns for soldiers, diplomats, the dancers in the brothel scene, and, of course, highly distinctive movement series invented for, and used only by, the characters of the Profiteer and Death.

Here again, as in " The Big City," the " spaceless " stage area used can become any place that the action needs to suggest. It is, in turn, barrack square, battleground or brothel : in some incidents, the sense of place relative to which the action is happening does not require definition. A stage has become again what it originally was in the Theatre— a place for action, and the need to help the performers put over the full weight of their work by painted, carved, or constructed setting simply does not exist. In the same way that the Elizabethan playgoer could take a hint from the costuming and the situation, and *believe* for the duration of any scene that that particular scene was a tropical forest, a cave in the ocean or a palace throne-room, so the stagecraft of these ballets, entirely subordinated to the business of dancing, places correctly in our attention as much sense of place as we need to have, through its particular emphasis on costume, properties and lighting only.

After we have seen the complete pattern of destruction, loss and misery which warfare imposes, and as Death dances his final tactical move and fades away into darkness, the emotional pressure of the ballet is suddenly shifted on to a different plane by the transference back to the conference table. We may read for ourselves whether this is a meeting convened to clear up the ruin caused by the incidents preceding, or whether it ironically points the process of the full-circling wheel. The music carries over stridently the few seconds between the fading-out of the figure of Death and the sudden relighting of the full stage, and we see again the green table with the ten diplomats in the identical attitudes of the close of the prologue. They signal their reappearance with, again, the shots in unison and, apologetically, tactfully, delicately, resume friendly relations and begin again their observations, heroics, protests and clichés as they take up their familiar places round the green table.

" A Ball in Old Vienna " is the oldest ballet of light mood in the Jooss repertoire, and dates from the same year as " The Big City," " The Green Table " and " Pulcinella." Its synopsis offers all the clues to the kind of emotional situation that will be revealed : " The gay and gallant life of the 1840's . . . sentimental intrigues of crinolined ladies and their ardent swains, to the entrancing rhythm of the waltz." For this ballet, Frederick Cohen arranged the score of the *Hofballtänze* of Lanner, the oldest and first of the nineteenth century school of Viennese waltz composers. The theme is of a ballroom occasion, a light escapade in which figure a Debutante and her admirer, an Eligible Young Man and his Sweetheart among the ball guests. The young ladies and the gallants flirt, pay compliments, and avoid, as far as possible, the interferences of the Debutante's guardians, a pair of spinster aunts, who have constituted themselves duennas of the occasion.

The slight subject-matter defines the weight of the situations in which the characters are involved, and the characters work within a more restricted technical patterning than Jooss commonly uses. As a foil to the other ballets of the same period of composition, it is an interesting revelation of Jooss' capacity to exploit an extant pattern of social dance on lines of his own. The spirit in which the earliest form of waltz was conceived, composed and danced has been preserved : the waltz of a century ago is here revealed as a dance allowing greater freedom of movement and pattern-making than the other dance forms of the time. By means of the formalised patterns of the dance action, the partners have ample opportunity of exploiting all the delicate amatory fencing that such an occasion could evoke in real life. There is a delicacy, a fluency and an air of youthfulness about this ballet (whose action is throughout almost entirely confined to rhythmic sequences firmly held in waltz tempo), which is a far cry from the tear-sodden sentimentality which is to-day the hall-mark of the waltz as it commonly occurs, either in the ballroom or on the stage.

The dancers of the slight and elegant episode, to Lanner's music, and in the costume of Lanner's day, are eager to flirt, to enchant or be enchanted. They are ready to fall in love, but they are not already heartbroken or loaded with inferiority complexes induced by one another's inconstancy, as in the contemporary convention of the song-waltz. These characters in the Jooss work stress gaiety, shyness and emotional simplicity ; qualities which are durable and which are still the prerequisite of the springtime of life—but with which the modern convention of the waltz, either in ballroom or on stage, has little connection. . . . *Autres temps, autres moeurs.*

When the Ballets Jooss returned to Paris in the spring of 1933 their repertoire included the three foregoing works and the earlier ballets of Jooss then extant. Of the dozen or more allegories, fables and dance-narratives which represented the summing-up of his successive discoveries in technique, each had served a certain purpose at a specific point, but the creation of these works did not qualify them for automatic inclusion in the repertory of the Ballets Jooss. There have been, for example, Kurt Jooss versions—or rather treatments of the identical subject-matter—of such ballets as " Fils Prodigue," " Le Bal," " Danses Polovtsiennes," " Coppelia," " Pulcinella," " Petrouchka," but they have no place in the canon of the Jooss Ballets to-day. As a theme, or rather a sort of master-theme with infinite ramifications, offering a dozen versions of the *leit-motif* of Youth in search of Love, there is the story which is the basis of " A Spring Tale " (1939) and which is found in a very early work, " Die Brautfahrt " (The Bride-Quest : 1925).

" Pavane," created 1929, touches upon the unreal life that goes on behind the façade of ceremonial and opulent magnificence which form courtly procedure. Ravel's fine merging together of the solemnity and simplicity which are characteristics of the pavane-form, with the plaintive intensity of the melodic line which he uses, have produced a work which is a high stylisation of Spanish musical form. The title offers all the incentive a choreographer requires, for the work *is* mourning music, a dirge for a dead lady, an elegiac outburst. Jooss demonstrates the dramatic possibilities latent in a fixed, traditional dance form as completely as he has done with the waltz in " A Ball in Old Vienna," in his use here of the pavane. Using the basic steps and body attitudes of the pavane-form, but adding his own inflexions of gesture and subtle variants of the timing, he has created a perfectly-proportioned miniature dance drama.

The synopsis condenses the entire narrative into these few words : " Her spirit imprisoned by the cold and pompous ceremonials of the old Spanish Court, the young Infanta seeks in vain to free herself, and succumbs finally beneath the burden of its elaborate etiquette." The coldness, the pompousness, the etiquette are remarkably realised, and set against them in sharp relief is the Infanta, centrepiece of this dance tragedy. It is tragedy because she is aware of the untouchable reserve and the profound pride which infect all the people in her retinue ; clothed with their dignity they are completely isolated from warmth and friendliness. She is aware of this and therefore realises that her struggle can never overcome their indifference, their inhumanity. She dances her protestation and her appeal, seeking only a little sympathy, a little human-ness. But the courtiers maintain their proper distance ; they tender the respect, the deference owing to her rank, protecting themselves all the time from life and from understanding under the camouflage of etiquette—the proper manner—the correct attitude.

The eight-part group of Court figures is used throughout in rigid, mathematically ordered patterns of step, gesture and inflexion all based on the precise and limited patterns of the pavane-form. This dance (in 4/2 time) has each step sharply articulated and kept separate from each other step. This introduces a mechanical harshness and coldness into the patterns, against which the Infanta's freely rhythmic and unformalised movement makes a remarkable characterising contrast. Though she lacks freedom and spontaneity of action, she desires them ; the other personages desire nothing further, so that every movement she makes comes up against the barrier line of their bodies—she can only exist within the narrow prison which they make around her. The set steps of pavane-form are so closely adhered to in order that all their implications of

52

stiffness, remoteness and rigidity may be carried through the characterisations of the Court figures. This has, quite involuntarily, given to anyone familiar with the classroom routine of five-position technique the impression of a gentle parodying of some of the unlovely muscular tightness and the mechanical accenting found in certain formal exercises in the classical *barre* routine. If an audience reads this suggestion, where it would be unobvious to the innocent eye, it can be but one more pointer to the contention that a work of art always holds all that its creator put into it, plus everything that the sympathetic spectator can see in it.

"Ballade," created in 1935, is another work based on a historical narrative and seems, to one spectator, a superb exercise in mime. The nuances of characterisation and plot incidents grow from the delicacy of the facial and gestural play, rather than from the formalised way in which the steps of galliard and passepied are used. A few words, quoted from an ancient song, serve as synopsis, and, indeed, sum up the whole story : " . . . The Queen, however, sent a poisoned bouquet to the young Marquise, who had been too much favoured by the King's attention." This ballet draws its dramatic strength from its revealing of motives, and precisely as in " Pavane " they are the motives behind Courtly behaviour. These two ballets indicate a (possibly unconscious) fascination in the actions and reactions of those people, at any social level, who are able to exercise practically unlimited power over others.

The emotional play of the simple plot is between the two couples, King and Queen, and Marquis and Marquise : courtiers are the usual decorative adjuncts to the highly formalised life which royalties lead, and woven around the individual psychological revelations of each principal character is a network whose strands are the inhumanity and heartlessness of almost every participant in this pathetic episode. Queenly dignity, in its mediæval interpretation, demands a suitably enormous punishment for the enormous offence of supposed intrusion upon the Queen's most intimate affairs. There is a partly - revealed, partly - unexplained emotional tension between the Queen and the Marquis : the most dominant characterisation is that of the Queen, who is, nevertheless, almost a static element in the action of the ballet. She is, at a certain level, one kind of sufferer, and the Marquis who suffers a violent loss,

undergoes torment of a different kind which reveals him as a character on another plane. He is the most completely rounded and warmly human person in the scene; which gives to his personality an almost Aeschylean cast, for he can be treated as a pawn of even less significance than his wife should he merit the Queen's disfavour. The true importance of the King's interest in the Marquise is probably of far less magnitude than that given it by the Queen's ruthless assessment of the situation. In fact, one senses a latent sub-plot, never given precise definition by the choreographer in which the whole occurrence narrated grows out of the Queen's desire to impress on the Marquis the range of her awful power. There is a mordant and a desperate note in this work, which is underlined by the casual way in which the decorative and symbolic appurtenances of chivalry are revealed as so much dross on the surface of the events leading to the vile climax. It is as truly in keeping with our knowledge of these types of historical personage, as are any of the recorded violences practised by the Borgias on the objects of their mistrust. John Colman's music is a series of free variations on the mediæval French song from which Kurt Jooss derived the story. The homogeneity of action and stagecraft is furthered by the costumes designed by Heckroth, which provide a clue to those personalities masked by the proud and suave faces, rather than give that pictorial magnificence one associates with the dresses at a mediæval European Court.

Kurt Jooss had made at Essen, in 1931, a ballet on the theme of the Prodigal Son. The music by Prokofiev, and the libretto by Kochno, were those used by Balanchine when making "Le Fils Prodigue" for Diaghilev in 1929. In 1933, when the Ballets Jooss undertook its first world tour, a completely new ballet on this theme formed one or the new works. For this work he used a score written collaboratively by Frederick Cohen, and adapted the parable to give him a plot suitable for his style of dramatic manipulation. This ballet subject was made into a second version in 1939, still to Cohen's music and with dresses by Dmitri Bouchène. It may be of interest to note that the Diaghilev Ballet's scheme of decor by Rouault, together with Prokofiev's score, formed two of the elements in yet another choreographic version, which Lichine, in 1939, made for the De Basil Ballet.

The two choreographers, Balanchine and Jooss, have both concentrated on the simple and strongly dramatic elements of the old parable: in each case the climax is the moment of the Son's prostration before his father, and the swift finale depicts the act of forgiving. Balanchine has pointed out that this story (the first half only of the biblical narrative) makes the perfect type plot for a ballet of dramatic action: "Once there was a man who had everything; then he had nothing—finally he had everything again." In Jooss's treatment the accents placed on the story give it a different rhythm from that found in Balanchine's or Lichine's versions, though they use substantially the same plot outline.

Kochno introduced two companions for the Son, who accompanied him on his journey and his lurid adventures. Jooss makes a new character in the Mysterious Companion whom the adventuring Son treats at first as an enemy and fights against; he is vanquished and the Companion poses as a friend who is able to set him on the road to success. But when the Son has achieved glory and is crowned a King, his success begins to corrupt him and the Companion opposes him and leads the opposition which overthrows him. After the Son has suffered complete abasement and starts his homeward journey, truly penitent, the Companion accosts him again but is repulsed.

For this ballet the story's rhythm flows upward in a steep curve to the first act climax of the Son's investiture in robe and crown; it declines in accelerating tempo to the final incident of his humiliation and suffering; thence the emotional emphasis shifts to a different plane and in the calm, pastoral atmosphere of the home-coming episode the entire narrative sums itself around the focal point of the Father and Son relationship.

The music is, in the case of this ballet, a more colourful and rhythmically exciting score than in any other of Cohen's, and the work is given dramatic precision by Jooss's working to such admirable music. At the first break in the story we have seen the incidents of the departure, the meeting with the Companion, the two journeying to the City, and the Son's all-conquering progress therein. The perfect success story is told with a fine, vigorous sweep of dramatic movement in which the incidents of personal adventure form so many points of eddy, around which the swirl of atmospherics, the milieu, the secondary characters rotate, and we have, to borrow a term from a different craft, close focus and long-range shots perfectly superimposed, so that we are steadily aware of the larger picture which is taking shape and of the significant highlights which give it its æsthetic quality.

The unwinding of the success story is as violent and as effective in its speed as was the building up in the first act. The Son is attacked by his followers, stripped of robe and crown and finally escapes only by merging himself in the crowd of his pursuers. This is a half-turn of Fortune's wheel, and though defeated he is not yet in despair. Friendship is offered him by two strange women and this he accepts. They are harlots, and whilst he relaxes in their company and with their associates, the Mysterious Stranger of the outward journey reappears and presents him to the Queen of the Harlots. He accepts her favours, and immediately the Stranger denounces him as the fallen tyrant; even these people hold him in contempt and beat and revile him. Only when he has eaten the fruit of bitterness, only when complete disillusion has overcome him, is he able to see the enormity of his sins. Pride and ambition for power have guided him to the height he reached when Kingship was offered him; the same destructive elements have debased him to a level he had not known to exist. Penniless, sick and hungry, he journeys wearily towards home; once again the mocking Stranger appears, and the Son, by rejecting him, at last reveals that he has discovered himself. " . . . he finds his way home. Loving care awaits him and gives him new strength. The rhythm from which he fled with impatience as a youth comes back to the mature man as a radiant memory. He now does happily and from choice what he had hated doing under compulsion." So the closing words of the synopsis give the final picture. The story told has touched upon almost every problem, moral, intellectual and emotional, with which man is faced in his social relationships. There is no proselytising, no emphasis of praise or blame: one may go through a life in this way, rejecting love, ambitious and confident; one may achieve or miss worldly success. Conscience or Reason or Imagination—however we like to vary the symbolic nature of the Companion—may be a good guide or a bad one. If we need to be taught a lesson, we may learn from the hardships the

world imposes on us—or we may not. The certain thing, never yet disproved, is that however shameless, however vile, none of us is beyond love : the only reward worth having, the only prize unreachable through conscious effort. As the one constant value in the world, this fact of love as the final human identification, the only mark that really distinguishes us as a species entirely separable from the beasts of the desert and the forest, is here proved to us once again through that kind of unstressed statement that only Jooss can make in the medium of dramatic dance.

Between " The Prodigal Son " and the next work of similar scale and length (" The Mirror," 1935) Jooss composed " Johann Strauss, To-night ! " and " Ballade," both in 1935. The Ballets Jooss undertook a world tour extending through the winter of 1933 to the following midsummer and during this period Jooss transferred the school from its Essen headquarters to Dartington Hall.

On returning from the first extensive tour, the company was practically disbanded, and a nucleus of dancers on whom the new school and the company would be built up then went into residence at Dartington Hall, in Devon. The reconstituted company danced the whole existing repertoire in the newly-built Barn Theatre at Dartington in September of 1935, and immediately after began a second world tour.

The tours undertaken between the autumn of 1933 and early 1939 had brought the Ballets Jooss into more than two hundred European and American cities. This work was carried out by substantially the same company which Jooss had built up from the fresh nucleus at Dartington.

The existence of the Ballets Jooss has been naturally dependent on a school and training centre from which the company could be fed. As no school existed for the particular forms of tuition required for the Jooss method of dance-composition, Jooss has had to plan and organise and supervise such a school. This is the admirable arrangement so often postulated as essential for aligning the pedagogic with the creative occasion in Ballet : The Russian Ballet under Diaghilev consisted of dancers who had been brought up along these lines. The schools existed not just to train and educate dancers, but to train and educate dancers for pre-arranged dancing careers in a highly-organised system of theatres.

The setting up of the Jooss-Leeder school and the headquarters of the Ballets Jooss at Dartington Hall brought to realisation Jooss's early dream of an academy of the arts in rural surroundings, and from this point in 1934 his work embraced every part of the direction of both school and company. He was training both dancers and dance teachers, as well as creating a repertory of works and quite frequently dancing in them. No theatrical method of our time carries more clearly the personal mark of its originator, high priest and chief executant.

At Dartington the Jooss precepts were given two-fold expression ; with Leeder as co-director he worked in the Dance School creating a vital pedagogic method for his system, and in addition he guided the development of, and provided works for, the Ballet Company. To this period, 1934-39, belong five ballets : of these " Ballade " has already had reference, and three are no longer in current repertoire. Two of the four—" The Mirror " and " Chronica "—are full length works with a content as significant as anything Jooss has yet made. " The Seven Heroes " (1933) and " Johann Strauss, To-night ! " (1935) call for a brief note.

" The Seven Heroes " had immediately preceded " The Prodigal Son," and was in circulation for only a few months of 1933 and 1934 ; a new version of the tale with fresh costumes was made in 1937. The story was based on a Grimm fairytale, and in its original shape was partly inspired by Jooss's admiration for Purcell. (One of the happiest of the early collaborations had been the production in 1926 at Münster of Purcell's " Dido and Aeneas." This joyful labour undertaken by Jooss, Heckroth and Schulz-Dornburg, the Münster resident conductor, was considerably lightened by the active assistance and enthusiasm of Professor Edward Dent, at that time visiting Münster, who worked daily with Jooss on the text. This occasion marked not only the effective introduction of Purcell's music to contemporary Germany, but also the first professional theatrical production ever given to this work.) For their comic subject of Ballet, Jooss and Cohen decided on Purcell's theatre music, and Cohen selected a three-part suite which, with interpolations to cover the transitions, made an appropriate continuity for the earthy tale. This peasant lark in a mid-European setting with bucolic love-making, a chorus of nagging wives, and the gang of henpecked husbands who went out on a great bear-hunt, is one of the few instances of the naïvely comic in Jooss's work. It was for too long out of circulation, and it is good news that it is back again in the repertoire.

" Johann Strauss, To-night ! " was a farcical episode of ghosts come back to earth for a night's gaiety, accompanied by the Devil and his Grandmother. The setting was an approximation of the story-book Vienna, and a free adaptation was made by F. A. Cohen of the music of "Ritter Passmann," one of the many operettas of the more prolific Strauss. The costumes by George Kirsta stressed the farcical and colourful nature of the happenings, and for some time the ballet endured as one of the small list of light and gay character ballets, which was, on the whole, a less successful integration of formal styles with Jooss's plastic and gesture than either " Ball in Old Vienna " or " The Seven Heroes."

" The Mirror," coming three years after " The Green Table," was another close-knit collaboration of the three who had made the first great dance-drama. Frederick Cohen composed the music, Hein Heckroth designed costumes and properties and Kurt Jooss developed, through the choreographic forms, his ideas and reflections upon the still un-

Z80

Brazilian

Mr Zullig

Country Daughter

Z82 Country Gentleman

283 (Dream cont)

Mr Alexander

Dream

Country Mother

House keeper

Town Daughter
(Coach)

284 Coachman
Bolton  Miss Nesch

resolved problems of post-war adjustment. His synopsis reads, " ' The Mirror ' reflects the confusion and worries, the despair and the hopes of post-war mankind struggling to escape from the moral, social and political consequences of his own folly."

The action centres upon three comrades of war, different social types who, from the impersonal anonymity of soldiers, have revealed to each other their humanity and affection. They are typified as the Man of Leisure, the Middleclass Man and the Labourer. The opening scene deals with the disorder and chaos which lie upon the scene of warfare after hostilities have ceased ; the comrades-in-arms help one another in their struggle to escape, and we next see them as civilians resuming their pre-war patterns of life. For the first two there is celebration, leisure and entertainment : for the Labourer a prompt return to his slum home and his labouring. The disorganised condition of the post-war European scene with the new social acceptance of vast numbers of " unemployables " is the theme which now emerges and dominates the action. The forced idleness of unemployment breeds a despair in the Labourer, which leads to the breaking-up of his home and the abandoning of his wife. The bourgeois Young Man is troubled by the lack of interest of his kind of people in the sufferings and misery around them : his remedy is to attempt to unite bourgeois and proletarian feeling in a movement opposed to the rich men's capitalism. But his background and antecedents only arouse suspicion and hostility among the poor he seeks to lead. It is later, after we witness an interposed incident of the fate of the Labourer's deserted wife become a woman of the streets, that the bourgeois Young Man emerges with powers of leadership which enable him to guide a revolutionary movement opposed to the inheritors of wealth. Revolution breaks out and the resulting violence effects the breakdown of all social order, and misery is every man's portion.

The three comrades, back again on level terms, realise their inability to control or limit the far greater chaos which has engulfed them. The key to a solving of the problems is the re-awakening of understanding, and the outcast wife of the Poor Man sets an example by revealing the unselfishness of her love. The three comrades can face the world again, rid of their fears and hatreds by the revelation of the power of understanding, sympathy and mutual regard.

However much this work may seem to state the political complications in a simplified manner, its importance, and the idea most persuasively projected from it, lies in the enormous humanitarian truth embodied in the preaching of understanding and tolerance. Kurt Jooss is, as an individual, far too much the realist to imply, choreographically, that the political generalisations which made the broad framework for this parable are to be read as politically precise or practicable. This work grew fairly obviously out of Jooss's personal memories of the despair and greyness, lit only by an occasional outburst of hysterical and unfounded optimism, which marked the city life he knew in the early and middle 'twenties. It was in this period that Laban had been set up in his experimental studio-theatre in Hamburg, using buildings in the grounds of the Hamburg Zoo. Here Jooss was working with him, and knew the financial instability—and the accruing psychological instability—of the period in which paper money could lose ninety per cent. of its value between breakfast and lunch. Jooss's part-time occupation as a teacher of ballroom dancing at this period was, at times, the certain means of guaranteeing that he could pay for a meal in a restaurant. In some respects it was a ballet that *had* to be made ; after the artistic and the commercial success of " The Green Table," this subject-matter, second only in importance as a theme to that of the first great work, was the obvious major contemporary theme for symbolic presentation in dance-drama form. The work lacked the dramatic tension of " The Green Table " and though its patterns of violent action, and particularly the " signature " movements of some of the principal characters, were thrilling and lovely to watch, there was lacking that complete interlocking of symbolism and action-reality which gave such overwhelming dramatic weight to every movement of " The Green Table " and to each of the emotional climaxes within the framework of " The Prodigal Son."

" Chronica " was made during 1937 and 1938, an ominously significant time for a creative artist burdened with a strong social sense : and was first performed early in 1939 at Cambridge. It is arranged closely to a complex libretto, and tells a story of a strong man's achievement of power, how he used that power and what evil followed. The chief characters are Fortunato, the stranger who assumes dictatorship, Ferrone, the *condottiere* of the town and Andrea, the leader of the nobles; Andrea's sister, Clarissa, and Filippo, the Clerk, are the rest of the necessary personages for the involved plot. In synopsis the story is as follows : Fortunato comes a stranger into the town and finds men of similar ideas and tastes in Ferrone the *condottiere*, Andrea the nobleman, and Filippo the Town Clerk. Between them, they persuade the townsmen to accept Fortunato as their leader, and Andrea's sister, Clarissa, falls in love with him. As ruler, Fortunato seeks to bring order and prosperity and imposes his will on the people to such effect that an opposition, led by Andrea, is formed. This is betrayed by Filippo, who dies a traitor's death. Clarissa, seeking to intercede with Fortunato, discovers that even in her love she is watched by her lover's bodyguard, and loses her reason. This event shakes Fortunato, who tries to undo the disaster he has set afoot. Ferrone, disobeying Fortunato, is slain by Fortunato's hand ; but the soldiers are already marching to crush Andrea and the resistance, and to stop them Fortunato throws himself on their weapons : by thus sacrificing his life he redeems the city from the evil he has brought upon it.

The ballet is in three acts, the first occupied with the coming of Fortunato, his alliance with the town's leaders, his meeting with Clarissa and, finally, the townsmen's acceptance of him as ruler. Act two deals with the planning of the new order, its carrying out and the harshness that followed. Andrea, alarmed by the turn of events, pleads with Fortunato to restore the people's liberty ; this is refused and Andrea and Fortunato part. The third act begins with Andrea creating an opposition which is discovered by Ferrone and Filippo, the latter being caught and killed as a traitor. Clarissa's attempt at intervention, her madness and Ferrone's departure to crush the opposition lead to the moment of revelation for Fortunato. The climax is developed through Ferrone's rejection of Fortunato's authority, and his death, Clarissa's accidental death at the hands of Ferrone's troops and, finally, Fortunato's self-sacrifice in order to prevent the clash between guards and townsmen.

The action of the ballet falls easily into the formal dramatic order of (1) explanation and preparation of main situation, (2) development of main situation and its reaction upon the principal characters, (3) resolution of main situation into a series of tragic events, crowned by a climax of the deaths of the principal protagonists, these occurring in ascending order of characters and each proceeding from an unexpected but plausible turn of the plot. As psychological drama, this work is a very fine achievement, the actions of the characters spring from impulses clearly revealed and which we know to be true ; as types we know their parallels, from experience or accurate report as they occur in our time and in our society. Even as type characters of the historic period of the story, they ring true : Ferrone has the qualities of such a fifteenth century *condottiere* as the historians of mediæval Italy record, and the narrative holds a true pattern of behaviour such as we can note to-day, given approximately similar situations for the working of ambition.

The movement used, by a precise arrangement of signature patterns, gave living force to the dancers' actions, and the use of geometric type groupings enabled Jooss to display his skill in suggesting the multitude by the microcosm to a degree equalling the achievement in " The Green Table." The story, whilst veiling a contemporary political allegory under its historical cloak, held much more than a hard, ironic comment on the inevitable fate of dictators—even when these persons aspire to nothing more than a benevolent despotism. It was the parable of all men who succumb completely to the lust for power, and lose their humanity so that even those who would give them love and companionship are rejected. Bouchène's costumes were full of historic reference to the period through their use of symbolic decorations and their contrasting of differing textures of material. They gave grace or dignity to all the characters, and with Goldschmidt's music, created perfect technical instruments to support and enrich the other technical instrument of dance, in which Kurt Jooss created one of the great dance dramas merging clear dramatic event with exciting movement and outstandingly beautiful costume.

The other work of the same period (1938-39) was the final Jooss crystallisation of the ideas given shape in a ballet as far back as 1925, when " Die Brautfahrt " (The Bride-Quest) was made on an arrangement of Bach, Rameau and Lully, and danced by the first group constituting the *Neue Tanzbühne*. Probably a good deal of the essence of " Die Brautfahrt " is contained in " A Spring Tale," which is an allegory, a symbolic relation, of the loveliness and joy of youth and the unhappiness which too often is made for young people by the domination of their elders. These are the three principal parties to the story : the Prince and his friends, a Knight and a Huntsman ; then the Queen, Princess and Attendants of the Women's Court ; lastly, a group of Nature characters and spirits led by a Wondrous Hermit. The four acts deal with the adventures of the Prince and his companions when he sets out in search of a bride. They come to the Women's Court, where they are formally received, the Prince gets no encouragement for his suit from the Queen, and the Princess does not realise that she is—or ought to be !—in love with him. The Prince goes off, and when the Court retires for the night, the Hermit appears and guides the Princess away into the woods. Lost in a storm and terrified by the wood spirits, she is found by the Prince who escorts her home. In the last act, the Prince returns to the Court to plead again for the Princess's hand, she recognises him as her deliverer, and everything turns out as it should in a fairy story. For Jooss has meant that this tale shall be full of meanings, and they must be the meanings that anyone witnessing it may care to see ; the story can be accepted, quite literally, as a tale of fancy, and it can be read at any other level of meaning than the obvious, surface level. His synopsis reads : " This ballet is a fairytale. And like all real fairytales it has a two-fold meaning : one for children, another for grown-ups. There is a Prince, a Knight and a Huntsman—perhaps they represent the force, the strength and the unconscious desire for love which fill the heart of youth ? Then there is a Queen, a Mistress of Ceremonies and a Princess—they could represent the bitterness of lonely women, and the tenderness and dreams of a lovely maiden. There is, too, a haunted wood in which are revealed the strength and enchantments of Nature. Finally there is the figure of the Wondrous Hermit who is the good which lies deep in all creation, and who, in his kindness, leads on to the happy ending." The music for this work was, again, composed by F. Cohen, working with Jooss and amongst the dancers while in residence at Dartington ; and Heckroth (also a member of the Dartington Hall organisation) who had designed for the greater part of Jooss's ballets, produced some of the finest symbolic costumes, and a number of superbly beautiful ones, for this tale. The first act dancing for the men is of a rare simplicity of shape—vigorous, clean and exciting : by contrast, the Women's Court is peopled with figures who shuffle, totter and shamble about as though any kind of physical spontaneity were denied them. Their nervous conventionality is summed up in the figures of the Mistress of Ceremonies and a grotesque sort of eunuch who is the Butler. In the night, after the Princess has been put to bed (with the entire female Court sleeping on the floor on guard around her) the Hermit steals in at the window and guides her away. She may be spirited away in sleep and wake only during her disturbing woodland adventure, or the whole nocturnal episode may be but a dream, so that when she next, in her waking life, sees the Prince, she recollects her dream and realises that she has fallen in love with him. The story has some *longueurs*, and when emphatic use is made of certain tricks of repetition this, while underlining the character, or an attribute that a group of characters may share, does not help the easy flow of that part of the story. But once the plot has become clear, the stylising of gesture, of facial acting, of dance, of sheerly grotesque movement, make for that intensive and inexhaustible revelation of character which is part of Kurt Jooss's purpose. In its physical pictures of movement it has the bright, clean openness of a fairy-tale illustration : simple and very slightly varied signature patterns for each of the principal characters make them easy of identification to the child or the unsophisticate who sees the work. Like many other simple yet profound stories, it can be a delightful experience for children of all ages. The occurrence of this work in the Jooss repertory propounds the desirability of him creating further ballets based on the widely-known fairytales of our European culture. For this form of theatrical representation is one of the obvious methods by which they can be given that symbolic clarifying they need (to have memorable meaning to the child mind) and which they seldom receive. There is no danger of a familiar story being overlaid with one fixed symbolic interpretation. Treated as imaginatively as Kurt Jooss treated the substance of " A Spring Tale," they will suggest to the receptive personality, through the broad symbolic references lightly touched upon, a whole range of allegorical and intensely *personal* reflections.

" Chronica " and " A Spring Tale " were the last pre-war works ; the autumn tour of 1939 was carried out, and at the end of the year the company made its sixth Atlantic crossing to fulfil contracts for touring in North and South America during which a repertory of nine ballets was presented. To these a ballet by Agnes de Mille, " Drums Sound in Hackensack," was added in 1941 ; this was a work based on the early colonial life of the seaboard states. Once in America the company was isolated there, and during almost three years' working travelled some thirty thousand miles over the whole continent. Conditions were not always easy, and it was an achievement in which everyone shared to maintain that cohesion necessary to keep a living repertory in continuous existence. The bonds which hold the people of this company to one another, and to Kurt Jooss, are strong ; the interim during which he was separated from them might have proved an unbridgeable gap to many choreographers. Activities at Dartington Hall had occupied both Leeder and Jooss through the first winter and spring after the company's departure. During that summer they were compelled to move away from that part of England, and the centre from which the Ballets Jooss has worked since returning to this country is now Cambridge.

Very shortly after the return from America the company, strengthened with new personnel, was rehearsing fresh ballets. The first of these was almost exactly four years later than the preceding ballet from the hand of Jooss. " Company at the Manor " was a light-hearted frolic, a tale of young love overcoming misunderstandings. The period was early nineteenth century, the setting a small country house, the music (alarmingly, to some) a Beethoven sonata arranged for pianos. Doris Zinkeisen's dresses and stylised furnishings were highly effective in the creation of period-atmosphere for this entertaining work, which carried no overt or implied critical comment on the scene portrayed or the situations revealed. An Early Victorian household of mother, son and daughter invite their town friends to visit the manor ; the son, Oliver, is in love with the daughter of the town household, Cecilia. But a dashing Brazilian gentleman comes to pay a call on the family and loses his heart to her. Demurely she accepts the situation in which, it is indicated to her,

she has a very proper place—as Armando's betrothed. But in a dream Cecilia sees a shadowy ballroom, and from among the dancing figures emerges Oliver who reveals that he dearly loves her, and pines for her. When she wakes she is afraid and unhappy. The family take Armando with them on the visit, and at first sight of Oliver's sister, Charlotte, his volatile affections are transferred to her. This *volte-face* removes the barrier between Oliver and Cecilia and the four young people happily adjust the situation to their true desires.

63

The characters, partly circumscribed by the nature of the story, are clearly established at their first appearance; and their exponents, as highly skilled actor-dancers, exploit their special sort of virtuosity in a gallery of portraits, but one remove from the pages of Jane Austen. Every eyebrow tells a story, and the arching of a wrist carries significance among these mannered, poised and fully alive people. No piece of solo or duet dancing, or a passage of mime, detached from its context in a Jooss ballet, is appreciable as a balletic *morceau*, but in this work the satanic charm of Armando, the self-conceit of the Coachman, and the smooth duet patterns of the dream sequence, have their own appeal as comic or lyric decorations to the wholesome story.

Two years' active preparation preceded the first performance of Kurt Jooss's most recent ballet, " Pandora," which was first produceed in Cambridge early in 1944. The extraordinary quality of this work rests on its powerful theatricalism (the manner in which a high output of emotional stimulus is maintained throughout), and on its sustained arousing of correspondences and references out of active memory and the subconscious, which are projected on to the mirror of the mind. We are emotionally moved and are aware of what is moving us; the processes of experiencing, and of weighing experience, happen simultaneously. The basis of the work is the Pandora myth, but substantially varied by Jooss to provide an infinitude of imagery and allegorical suggestions. His synopsis reads : " Pandora, a beautiful woman without a soul, is sent by the jealous gods with the gift of a box to mankind. Deceived by Pandora's beauty men strive to possess and open the box, but when they succeed, instead of happiness, all Evils and Miseries are let loose from it. In contrast with Pandora stands Psyche, the personification of the soul and of unselfish devotion. The ballet shows mankind, torn in the ever-recurring struggle between the material and spiritual forces represented in these two figures."

This résumé is a stenographic note, as it were, showing to what extent the original myth has been varied : it in

no way prepares one for the magnitude of the forthcoming assault on the senses and the mind. A clue to the measurement of this ballet can be found in a brief investigation of some trends in ballet-making within recent years. The content which forms the expression-basis of a work of art is usually as revealing of the artist's background and conditioning, as it is of the particular impulse to which he reacted in making the work of art. The political acumen of sixteenth century London apprentices and students is revealed, and the awakening interest in the vast unknown spaces of the earth is foreshadowed in, for instance, the plays of Shakespeare. The better part of our literature of the late seventeenth and eighteenth centuries is imbued with contemporary concern for matters of Form, Style and Rational Order, which were a philosophic colouring of the period's thought derived substantially from Pascal's and Descartes' mathematical researches and Newton's scientific formulations. During the inter-war period of this century, European thought generally has been dominated by memories of the 1914-18 war and its tangible aftermath— the world depression begun in 1929, the rise of the dictators, the high incidence of un-

employment, etc. Contemplation of these happenings has promoted a fear that another major war would begin in our time, and the body of thinking concerned with this grim prospect has stimulated both direct and oblique comment from the majority of creative artists in the period. Even the more strident forms of escapist art, and nearly all " kitsch," can be related to their creators' belief that certain political realities simply did not, in fact, exist.[10]

In the sense that all human activity is but a series of reflections of the images projected from the dominant political systems, so is the converse true ; and all forms of response to, and reaction against, the tragic farce of European politics from 1929 to 1939, are displayed in the arts, religions and leisure-patterns which make up contemporary European culture. During recent years a high proportion of creative artists in Ballet have shown an interest in two striking themes. Each theme can be defined in a phrase which could serve as sub-title to half-a-dozen ballets equally ; these phrases are : Man in search of his Soul, and The conflict between Good and Evil within Man. The first theme may have occurred in Ballet earlier than we suspect, but its first notable appearance in our time is in Fokine's " Chopiniana " (1908). When we recall the idea behind a whole series of ballets made in the 1930's, it will be apparent that this—generally unconscious—desire to identify Self with something larger than Self has come to the surface of the stream of European art in a very marked way, and forms a significant footnote on the Existence of Artists and the Importance of Art in a Machine Age. For five works by outstanding choreographers made, or given revival, between 1930 and 1939 : " Apparitions " (Ashton), " The Well-beloved " (Nijinska), " Symphonie Fantastique " (Massine), " Paganini " (Fokine) and " Transcendence " (Balanchine), are all concerned with a principal character in search of an influence, an ideal, or a supernormal being on whom he can rest and from whom he can draw the strength he personally lacks. Their differences are of Style, not of Matter.

The other recurring theme (the Struggle theme) which is equally significant but much less depressing to contemplate, is found in ballets by many choreographers and under several idealistic and symbolic disguisings. In these works, by the nature of the balletic form, the struggle has to be rendered literal. The only identification required of the spectator is to note that " Good " wears white and " Evil " black—or whatever else ; after this point all attention can be concentrated on the amount of Evil opposed to a given amount of Good, and in noting the atmospheric variations with which the different choreographers invest the narrative.

In " Pandora " the theme is an enormous amplification of the first simple idea in the synopsis, as mystifying and yet as stimulating, as life itself. The struggle is not between two external elements for the domination of man ; Good and Evil do not exist as opposed entities, but each is a part of human behaviour at any level of cultural development or understanding.   In ourselves we constantly feel the tension between them; when we think they are dormant we may with extreme self-confidence assume that the equation has been solved—only to find that yesterday's Good has become to-day's Evil.   Only the most scrupulous questioning of our inmost selves can maintain the proper tension between these forces, whether we define them as the Material and the Spiritual, or the Instinctive and the Intellectual. To live is to accept this necessity to struggle, for only by so doing do we have liberty, and the highest form of liberty is the liberty to be completely human.   For this we fight every day, maintaining a system of checks and balances on our instincts and our intellects.

The action of the ballet is borne by six principal characters and two groups, the latter representing the common men and women of the earth and the evil powers loosed by Pandora.   The principals are : Pandora, the gods' messenger, soulless and beautiful and wholly destructive ; The Youth, innocent and unprejudiced, symbol of the simplicity and the desire for happiness in us all ; Psyche, the Good in man ? or the whole of humanity in opposition to the evils sent by the gods, who " kill us for their sport " ?   The Go-Getter, who desires only personal advancement and the winning of earthly riches ; The Strong Man, symbol of pure-heartedness and courage ; The Mother, the dominant feminine character type.   The group of the People comprises young and old, both men and women, all equally capable of sacrifice and greed, each a potential sinner as much as a saint ; each carries in himself qualities with which the others are, at different times, in sympathy and opposition.   The acts are separated by a short interval, and this falls after the episodes of the winning of Pandora's box, the loosing of the monsters and their triumph over man : the monsters accept Pandora as their mistress and crown her.   The second act shows the world desolated by the evils, and suffering has become everyone's lot ; yet even those who have suffered already make further errors and create fresh evils because they betray their children to the Machine God.   The Youth holds steadfast to the vision of Psyche and thus betrays no one.   The power and integrity of the figure of Psyche is the crowning revelation of this work.   The recital of the narrative can convey little of the meaning that every separate incident projects, for every character is not only a particular symbol of a state, quality or entity, but also assumes, as it were, mask-like, a series of different symbolic faces at various points in the action.   Each one of them is the sum of certain tendencies in all living people, and is also each individual one of us at different stages of our spiritual growth.   We see first, the crowd searching for something to worship, whether within or external to themselves matters not.   Pandora appears and fascinates them ; all follow her except the Youth who searches more patiently, more arduously.   Psyche appears to him, and the Youth is drawn to her, but cannot touch her, and is mystified.   The crowd reappears, the Youth tries to tell of his vision and is repulsed.   Pandora shows her magic box and the two most vital elements among the people, the Strong Man and the Go-Getter, contend for it.   To the Strong Man's courage the Go-Getter opposes cunning and gains the prize.   He opens the box and a horde of monsters is loosed upon the earth.   The Strong Man is crushed trying to thwart them ; after wreaking evil on all they foregather to crown Pandora their triumphant ruler.

The second act opens with a great tragic lament, the mothers of the world who have seen the fruit of their love sacrificed to the monsters.   In a vision they see their dead sons who have fallen on all mankind's battlefields.   The new gods seek their allegiance and the Mothers accept them, thus putting a barrier for ever between themselves and their children.   This betrayal is the crime which generation after generation commits, the older people unthinkingly choosing the easy way out of responsibility.   Into a lamenting world, peopled anew, comes again the Youth—eternal symbol of hope, the child reborn, man in his pristine innocence.   Pandora appears and strikes down the people, but she cannot vanquish the Youth who has armoured himself with the vision of Psyche.   Pandora is banished, and the world comes to life again. . . .

No suggestion is made that any final solution has been found.   The fight must go on, and will always be as strenuous and as exhausting as in the past.   Fresh battalions of monsters will assail us from time to time, and perhaps if we preserve some of the Youth's simplicity and his belief in the power of Psyche, we can make bearable the struggle. Yet again, we can read in the work a penetrating because unforced comment on our eternal need of love : with " love " meant not as a romantic allegory on sexuality, nor even particularly as that neighbourly good feeling which enables us to keep the peace happily, but meant as a willingness to tolerate and understand all men, stripping ourselves of prejudice and preconception, and accepting all human creation as part of ourselves, to know with our hearts as well as with our minds.

What might be identified as the sum of humanitarian thinking—of all hard-headed assessment by a thousand thinkers around the problems of making the world a fit place for humanity—is in some way drawn upon in this work. Not, of course, that similar observations have escaped mention in the Theatre before now.   All the power of dramaturgy has been bent to giving utterance, at various times and in many forms, to every part of the great question to which Kurt Jooss refers throughout " Pandora."   But no work, outside the field of acted vocal drama, has before attempted to show through this high concentration of acceptable symbolism, the whole macrocosmic picture of humanity enmeshed in the entirely human, and therefore infinitely dramatic, struggle to know itself.

The outward form, of movement designs in three dimensions, with which Jooss invested this work shows a simplicity

Hein Heckroth 1943 "PANDORA" Ballet JOOSS

and breadth which have only been attainable by continuous examination, rejection and refining. The signatures of the principal characters, but especially the Youth, Pandora and Psyche, are movement-series elevated to a new and higher power of revelation. The ballet suggests an increase in Kurt Jooss's creative power, particularly in projecting the life-size character, who is at the same time seen in a sort of fourth-dimensional shape, as a larger-than-life creature containing each and all of us. This is the quality making for the closest identification between spectator and performer, and is the mainspring of the shattering catharsis to which the unprejudiced spectator is subjected.

Music for this ballet was composed by Roberto Gerhard, whose work is properly strident and harsh for whole sequences, and yet flowers into superb melody at those points where a telling melody crowns or rounds out the establishment of a mood or an incident. Hein Heckroth, still able, after fifteen years, to think with Kurt Jooss's mind, designed costumes which reached a fresh plane of symbolic value and beauty. Emphasised or shadowed by the lighting the colour range was always alive and sustaining to the dance shapes. Only one single-colour dress was used, Psyche's white robe; Pandora was clad in a robe of crimson, white and purple, with a head-dress of snakes, and the monsters crowned her with a grinning death's-head from which arose white crystalline spikes. Against these were the two-and three-coloured garments for the earthly people using black, chocolate, pink, lilac, sage, saffron and electric blue. The monsters were a surrealist vision of microcephalics and double-headed devils, led by a Machine Monster of which the head was a gargantuan Stillson wrench, the hands set-spanners and the legs enormous valve-springs.

This completes the list of Kurt Jooss's ballets to date. The first works by other choreographers who may use this system will emphasise its practicable nature (in showing that it is not simply a personal expression device peculiar to one man), and will also gradually reveal the many expansions that can be made into fields of expressible ideas differing from those of Kurt Jooss. The one ballet made by a non-Jooss dancer has been "Drums Sound in Hackensack," which Agnes de Mille created on the company in America in 1941. Miss de Mille has both Classical Ballet training and considerable experience as a dancer in forms of Modern Dance; how far she succeeded in using the idiosyncrasies of the Jooss-trained dancers to give expression to her New England story cannot now be reckoned, as the work was only given during part of the American engagement during 1941-42. The first ballets by new choreographers are "Sailors' Fancy" by Sigurd Leeder, and "Le Bosquet" by Hans Zullig.

Sigurd Leeder has been one of Kurt Jooss's closest collaborators since the time when both worked together with Laban in Hamburg. He has contributed enormously to the teaching method, and has made ballets which were danced chiefly by the students when at Dartington Hall. In a way it was inevitable that he should be the first choreographer, other than Jooss, for the Ballets Jooss. "Sailor's Fancy" was presented by the company in its first season after the return from America, and is described as a farce in five scenes. The first and last of these show the home port of the sailors, their preparations for a voyage, farewells to families, and what happens on the return from abroad. The three internal scenes are the milieux of their adventures in different foreign places with three girls; in each place the three comrades vie with one another for the favour of the lady of the moment. The ladies are an Asiatic, a Spaniard and an African, and each of the sailors is the winner of a lady's affections in each case. Each receives a love token from her, and at the end of the voyage, having meanwhile forgotten their wives and sweethearts, they present their tokens as the personal gift each had chosen for his beloved. But the ladies see through the pretence and decline the gifts; the storms and tears which ensue—and the chastisement of the sailors—are of brief duration, and the work ends with forgiveness all round.

The chief interest of this work is the measure of its choreographic difference from, and similarity to, the remainder of the Jooss canon. We see for the first time in the work of another person the application of those principles of dance-creation which Jooss had laboured so long and so hard to define. "Sailor's Fancy" simply by having been brought into existence is proof that the idiom is a complete and integrated method which can stand upright without Jooss's personal support. Leeder's work, difficult material for a first ballet, carried some excellent movement-series, recognisably originating in Jooss but with a flavour not of Jooss. The exaggerated note required for the telling of this tale was struck in the characterisations of the sailors, and perhaps not fully enough stressed in the female characters. The men had athletic and obviously skilful dance sequences, and their team-work as a trio of cunning rogues was marked with self-possession and the ability to stress the comic possibilities of the situations in which they were placed. Martin Penny's arrangement of folk melodies—in the main some of the best sea chanties we have—was appropriate both in temper and in rhythmic suitability. This is the first work in the company's repertory created independently of Jooss, and demonstrates that a choreographic system (as well as a dance system) exists, and can be handed on just as successfully. Within its own terms the system is as rigorous as any other, and the more difficult to manipulate in so far as there is no accumulated body of traditional practice to which reference can be made.

The next choreographer to emerge was Hans Zullig, who created "Le Bosquet" (first produced January, 1945), and in so doing revealed that this choreographic system could lift the dramatic dance to a plane on which it could compare with the pure visual æsthetic of the classical-style Ballet. "Le Bosquet," to music of Rameau, and with

69

an eighteenth century setting, is based on the slightest of plots : in the midst of a summer day's festivities, a young lady, hostess of the occasion, dreams or recollects a similar occasion when her lover, now vanished, had been present. The slightest thread of story suffices to hold together the main occasion and the dreamed or imagined episode occurring within it. The work is astonishing for the mastery of the dance style it reveals, and also the personal inflections made by Zullig upon that style. This ballet could not have been created in anything but the basic Jooss style of movement with its revelation of the superb and continuous plasticity of every moment of dancing. Hans Zullig has shown, moreover, that an evocation of the eighteenth century Courtly scene can be made alive and beautiful on the contemporary stage through a non-traditional dance style. The great significance of the work—apart from the adult and matured conception of the subject-matter—is in the revelation of the choreographic capacity of a dancer raised entirely within and by the Jooss system : for Zullig has not only an awareness of the value of fluidity, continuous motion and natural stasis as choreographic elements, but shows just how much can be wrought from a thoughtful appraisal of certain factors of the classical dance style.

A further point of interest about "Le Bosquet" was the devising of decor for the work ; it is the only extant ballet using an all-over stage setting—not a complete wings-and-backcloth structure—but with backcloth and wings set observably against the familiar black surround. For the occasion and period of the ballet this setting seemed too conventional a picture and was somewhat wooden, rather than sylvan, in effect. The costumes included some beautiful designs though there was lacking a unified style of colouring and materials. As usual the lighting was superb, contributing atmospherically to the narrative, and æsthetically to the harmonies of colour and movement. Few first ballets have revealed such mastery of the elements of dance and acting, and a choreographic instinct so sure and controlled as " Le Bosquet."

V

THE VALUE OF JOOSS

KURT JOOSS has had the distinction of being the only choreographer outside the Classical Dance system who has created works on a scale comparable with those in traditional form and made them artistically and commercially successful. The test of success in this period since Diaghilev is the ability to stand comparison in the commercial theatre with all other forms of theatrical expression—as the older form of Ballet and the Jooss Ballets have done.

The Ballets Jooss has been created in our time from zero ; the zero point being that day on which Jooss decided that effective theatrical shape must be given to a new system of ideas about Dancing. The Modern Dance—offspring of a thousand tendencies, impulses and desires—already existed, it fell to Jooss to elevate it from a series of manifestations each centred on an individual, or a pair of performers, into a method with shape, definition, laws and a pedagogy. The new ideas about Dancing had grown, by canalisation through Laban's work and the work of his pupils, into the trying out of every sort of theatre-craft and dance-craft to make a form carrying the new conception of " the ballet of ideas." In brief, this meant the stressing of the importance of Content over Form, and this is probably the greatest controversial issue with which theatrical dance has yet been concerned. Little research into the history of Dancing since Renaissance days is required to demonstrate that nearly every dancer and choreographer has accepted unhesitatingly this idea that the manner of dancing is more important than the matter. The whole tradition behind Ballet is a tradition of style-influences : the historical figures in Ballet who have made an impression which has lasted have done so by propounding fresh methods of invigorating dance-style. The acquired riches which invest this traditional system have been, at various times, used imaginatively and powerfully to give expression to an idea which was the germ of the ballet. Yet the power to give complete dramatic expression to any kind of idea has been almost entirely lacking, simply because the whole apparatus had grown up through several centuries as a form of theatre *spectacle*.

The earliest ballets we know were purely spectacular, and this element of the *visual importance* rather than the *symbolic importance* of dance and decor and story has become firmly woven into the very texture of classical theatrical dancing.

This has meant that the considerable theatrical potentialities of spectacular dancing exist to be exploited, and those Modern Dancers who have dismissed Ballet as outworn or decadent have cut themselves off from much that could be of use to them, no matter how strong their reformist urges might be. Kurt Jooss, though his dancing and choreographic career grew outside the traditional system, has studied and trained in it, as part of that broad field of learning he had to master. His ability to compare objectively the different factors which govern both the traditional and the Modern Dance systems, has guided him to select or reject with discretion any technical point or acquired mannerism from either system. This is in fact the only logical way in which he could have set about devising his dramatic dance-method, as there existed no choreographer or dancer, with a vast range of experience, from whom he could learn ; he had to adapt and invent, experiment and reject, reform and consolidate his raw material from many kinds of Theatre, and from the larger scene outside the Theatre. It is by his skill in imaginatively building together elements from all the styles of Modern Dance, and from the classical Ballet, into his own unique method, that he has earned his present position.

The broad differences of physical method embodied in the older and the newer dance systems are, that in the classical school (whether Italian or Russian) the dancer has the body trained so that all the elements of motion—elevation, balance, speed, direction—are controlled from a point low down in the spine. The spine is a flexible shaft, which can be tensed into rigidity—and mostly is—and the limbs rotate around this shaft like spokes from a hub. To help the spine have this amount of rigidity the hips are set squarely at right angles to it, and this also helps, and is helped by, the full turning out of feet—which can only be reached by training into this setting of the hips. The beauties of movement which can be produced on this specially developed physical instrument are innumerable, but it is obvious that the same development of physique has made for that frontal presentation which is the sign of the classical dance, and which can never permit the dancer to move with that freedom which the Jooss method encourages. Through this freedom from a control situated at an unvarying point, the Jooss dancers can move in that way which stresses their existence (on the stage) as three-dimensional persons.

To simplify considerably, the Jooss method of training aims at ridding the dancer's body of automatic tensions during movement (automatic because ingrained through excessive physical development which has taken place along a set pattern of muscular controls—as in the five-position classical system). The movement, whatever its intensity or shape, must be created anew each time, and this happens because the system of training works to *release afresh the dancer's latent ability to dance* every time he performs.

To this end Jooss and Leeder have worked on a training system which embodies the harmony concept of physical relationships which Laban had evolved. This notion had been rediscovered (it seems scarcely likely that it had not been known and worked on before) through the patient analysis and research into mathematical and geometric teachings reaching as far back as Pythagoras, and first architected into a philosophical structure by Plato. To chide Jooss for rejecting certain felicitous tricks and line-revealing poses from the Classical method is to expose one's misunderstanding of his aims. To this new dance system the following observations apply ; they are but a small indication of its distinctiveness.

The Jooss dancer cannot be out of dancing while on the stage ; the static moments either for individuals or groups have significance as much as the moments of movement.

The Jooss dancer can be unstable if that quality is properly part of a movement he is making ; it is not noticed as disequilibrium because he is all the time moving, from the first step, into movement : *the Classically trained dancer is moving into position (through being trained always to make a certain finish he is anticipating that finish throughout his movement).*

The Jooss dancer reproduces the experience which makes the Symbol significant ; this is because training has prepared him to re-create the experience for theatrical purposes.

The Jooss dancer acts with a convincing intensity because his gestural training is based on natural laws of mimicry and expression.

The Jooss dancer creates a three-dimensional character because every movement is based on an appreciation of the exact psychological impulse governing behaviour, the movement sometimes simultaneously expressing physical action and the working of the character's mind.

The Jooss dancer reveals the psychological truth (as distinct from the moral truth) behind any action, and so draws an uninhibited emotional response from the spectator : what he does strikes the note of truth and this truth depends on his actions seeming *absolutely natural.*

For the distinction between what is natural and what theatrical is probably more ephemeral than we suspect ; there is ample material for reflection in Goethe's observation : " Art is called Art simply because it is not Nature."

The sum of a considerable amount of research into, and constructive thinking about, every aspect of theatrical dancing is apparent in the work of this company. Of all the systems based on that revolutionary movement, the Modern Dance, it most closely corresponds with the traditional form of Ballet in its theatrical apparatus. Its radical differences from both the Modern Dance and the Classical Ballet give it individual character as a system. Of the many inheritors of the torch of Duncan, a certain few have thought first, and danced afterwards, and have thereby produced work of some artistic merit; but in general, these dancers whether American or European use an apparatus for training and for expression which lacks the time-proved effectiveness of the Classical discipline, and the logical smoothness between ends and means which Jooss has introduced. All too frequently the ideological substructure of their work is defined by—and therefore limited by—the executive ability of the leading exponent of the system. Among both Modernists and Classicists the ideas of Jooss have spread less in America than in Europe.

Twelve years' continuous existence, for a repertory of distinctive character, has proved it theatrically successful; that theatrical success has only been achieved because audiences have known a need for a fresh method, whatever its technical form might be, that was concerned with present-day realities rather than with denying reality. The Classical Ballet and the Jooss Ballet are complementary. Neither of them in the present condition of the European Theatre stands to gain anything by the elimination—were that possible—of the other. It is already obvious that there are cross-references between the systems and there have been borrowings of both technique and ideas of expression. Kurt Jooss has borrowed from the older system both for training and expressive purposes. His works show that these borrowings are not used as so much plastic decoration, but are integrated with his own inventions of movement and gestural pattern. Both systems show equal scrupulousness about the choice of music, which has to be so much more than effective rhythmic accompaniment, and both show an awareness of the great symbolising function of Costume in the Theatre. Jooss has been the first choreographer to carry to their fullest present-day realisation the architectural and plastic qualities of stage-lighting, and this new concept of the function of stage-space must be reckoned to the credit of the Modern movement. Not through any direct contact with Kurt Jooss, but certainly because of his inspiration, we see the gradual introduction of socially significant ideas into the synopses of ballets here and there. But the method of that form which has been growing for five hundred years now is still *mainly* concentrated on spectacularism. Choreographers still embark on too many new works while under the domination of the concept of " Dancers " rather than " Dancing." While it is quite true that any ballet of quality is concerned with an idea, the idea is generally used by the choreographer to give emphasis to the current predilections about plasticity, or music-symbolism, or a new twist in story-telling. But the new story is told in the old way, visual emphasis of movement and colour, and the fresh exercise in plasticity or the symbolic stressing of the music has become a new way of doing an old job. The tendency even amongst thinking choreographers is to think of ideas as fertilisers, and not as new roots or grafts. Mostly they serve to promote a fresh flowering from a deep-planted root : rarely is the idea buried deeply enough to become a completely fresh stem bearing a new kind of flower and fruit.

This most marked contrast between the primary aims of the two dominant systems of Theatre Dance in our day, really stresses their complementary nature rather than their antagonism. The Ballets Jooss has emerged as the new dance system which, at some point after the collapse of the Romantic Ballet, was bound to be created. Once Isadora Duncan (and, in a different way, Loie Fuller) gained acceptance of their new ideas about the purpose of Dance, and the ways of making Dance freshly significant, the way was open for the development of something on the scale of the Ballets Jooss : something which challenged the assumption that the Classical Ballet had done, and was still doing, everything theatrically possible with the art of Dancing.

Forms of art continually undergo mutations which are induced by artists who experiment with new materials, with fresh imaginative uses of old materials, or who bring in new ideas on the comparative value of Form and Content in any projected work. These are unavoidable changes growing from the flexible nature of social, and particularly industrial, conditions. The work of Jooss, by no means completed, is the strongest mutation pressing upon the art of Ballet in our time, and is as proper a development for Ballet as was, for instance, the discovery of the aptness of " pure dancing "—Dance for the sake of Dance—which occurred in France in the eighteenth century. This shift of balance was induced by changes in the forms of theatre music wrought by the composers of the day. Yet because this new orientation was supposed to weaken the classic dance-forms it was condemned by the balletic purists at that time. When, and only when, the particular mutation which is embodied in the dance philosophy of Jooss has penetrated right through the structure of contemporary theatrical dancing will it have served its purpose.

The *Concours International de Chorégraphie*, at which " The Green Table " was first performed, was the means of launching the Ballets Jooss on its European, and ultimately, world career. After the strange interlude at the Casino de Paris, the company toured Germany through the winter, and followed this with a first foreign tour which embraced visits to Belgium, Holland and Switzerland, a further visit to Paris, and the arrival for the first time in London, in June 1933. About this time the entire Jooss organisation ceased its connection with the Essen Opera House. The Paris impresarios Leon Greanin and Arnold Meckel were interested in Jooss's work and had organised the first foreign tour. Together with Kurt Jooss they now took over complete responsibility for the whole organisation, and " Ballets Jooss " was formed as a self-supporting unit; henceforth it would be a theatrical company earning a living in the variable financial atmosphere of the commercial theatre. It was primarily Greanin, a former member of Stanislavsky's

Moscow Art Theatre, who, with determination and boundless devotion to the idea of "Ballets Jooss," steered the organisation with success through the many difficulties of the international theatre world. When, in 1935, the Dartington Hall Trustees took over responsibility for the company, Greanin became its General Manager on their behalf and for seven years directed the business affairs, both internal and external, of the group.

Kurt Jooss's ethical convictions and their practical consequences could not fail to bring him into strong opposition, both in word and deed, with Nazi thought and methods. In September, 1933, when the first tour was being prepared, news was conveyed to Jooss that his arrest and removal to a concentration camp was a matter of a few hours. With the friends constituting the group, including Heckroth who was Stage Manager, he escaped secretly the same night across the Dutch frontier, and even managed to bring most of their theatrical equipment with him.

Contact with Mr. and Mrs. Elmhirst, founders of Dartington Hall Trust, opened up the possibility of moving the school from Essen to England. In April 1934, Sigurd Leeder and the entire staff together with twenty-two students left Germany, and the Jooss-Leeder School was established at Dartington Hall. It was the first professional activity of the newly-formed Arts Department administered by Christopher Martin.

Kurt Jooss's early dreams of a rural academy of the arts—with all the benefits accruing from that unstrained concentration on work which town-living precludes—was now realised. The arrangement of the affairs of both the Dance School and the Ballet Company was under conditions which made possible the successful operation of both enterprises. The school drew pupils from all over Europe and America. While working on the elaborate curriculum they lived as members of a community, within the boundaries of the one estate they worked, played, fed, slept and dreamed.

75

Dance practice rooms, music rooms, theatre, art school, workshops, farms, etc., were parts of the same process—a communal effort at living and working with the minimum of irrelevant distraction, disturbance and wasted time.

The School trained its pupils in all branches of period and national dancing, including certain parts of the Classical Ballet training formulas; in theories of the harmony of form and the psychological basis of dance-expressionism, in the use of a dance script (Laban's notation) and in music. Improvisation and the creation of choreography, together with practical work backstage of the Theatre whereby stage-management, decor, the function of lighting, make-up, were all related to the art of Dance, formed part of this comprehensive training schedule. The company was fed from the School, and apprentice dancers were taught by finished dancers who were still actively engaged in a dance career. Ballets embodying the new concept of Dance were prepared under practically ideal conditions, as to length and gradation of rehearsals, careful planning of costume, lighting arrangements and ample trying out under complete theatre conditions. The lengthy intervals between tours and the idyllic conditions at Dartington kept the dancers in the best dancing state, occupied busily with rehearsal, exercise, teaching and the creation of new roles yet suffering none of the strains which grow from incessant travel and perpetual performance.

The transfer of the School, with its initial staff and a nucleus of twenty-three pupils, took place while the company was touring even further afield: Holland, America, Paris, London, Belgium, Switzerland, Italy, Vienna, Budapest, Poland and Scandinavia. The return from this tour was followed by a reorganisation of the company; not all the dancers could adapt their private lives to the conditions of the new milieu. They included at that time people of several nationalities with strong ties which they were not willing to break.

The process of setting up this system of teaching, training and organising the company occupied a full year, and not until the autumn of 1935 did the reconstituted company give the first performances of Jooss ballets in the theatre at Dartington Hall. A nine months' tour followed, which began in Manchester and ended in Paris, via Holland, Scandinavia, America and Switzerland. The original Ballets Jooss of 1933 had changed some of its personnel, but Elsa Kahl, Rudolf Pescht, Ernst Uthoff and others of the first wave of Jooss dancers continued with the company for many years. No Ballet company of this size and importance had toured so much of Europe before, and places were visited in which travelling Ballet had never before been known. Not only the European capitals but dozens of cities of every size in France, Holland, Scandinavia, Hungary, Roumania, Austria, Finland, saw the repertory of Jooss during the years 1934-39. The French provincial cities had been visited early in 1937, and the next year a tour was made of the English provinces.

The fact that the Ballets Jooss has penetrated to so many corners of this and the American continent has spread a far-reaching propaganda for Jooss's ideas. Internationally touring Ballet companies have been a comparatively new realisation partly necessitated by the fresh conditions under which Ballet has existed since Diaghilev's time. All the companies which have appeared in America have worked under a difficult system of one-night stands, whereby most American cities are served with touring violinists, lecturers, world-tenors and Ballet.

In Europe a different system of theatre-and-performer relationship exists and where the large-scale " Russian Ballet " companies are only marketable in capital cities and a few established pleasure centres, Jooss has been able to send his company to almost any city in which there was a theatre of five hundred or more seats. This has been possible because of the comparative numerical smallness of the Ballets Jooss company, and the fact that it has been able to operate on smaller financial guarantees than would cover the risk for the larger units, and until early in 1945, the musical department comprised, at most, three persons.

All the processes which were behind the successful running of this planned dance academy and touring Ballet company have depended, finally, on the type of person who became a Jooss dancer. Germans, Swedes, Poles, Swiss, French, English, Americans, Spaniards, Dutch, Austrians, Hungarians, Latvians and Esthonians have been on the list of the company from time to time. This practical internationalism has resulted in an all-European circulation of new theatrical ideas carried by an all-European congregation of dancers. The signature of the Ballets Jooss has been proclaimed a European signature, and in the world of the Theatre, that which is European is also world-wide.

The difficulties encountered by Jooss and Leeder during 1940 and 1941 when the company was abroad, and isolated for an incalculable period, did not change their determination that, somehow, the Jooss Ballet must go on and the new system of ideas be kept in circulation. The changes growing out of war-time exigencies made for a complete reshaping of Kurt Jooss's plans; these plans at present find realisation in the tours of the Ballets Jooss in Great Britain and the Continent, and the preservation of the nucleus of the school at Cambridge. When better conditions for working return, the line of research, experiment and training will continue; a Jooss-Leeder school and a Jooss Ballet company will continue to support one another, though probably from a different headquarters, and with a different background than the dancers knew during the years at Dartington in Devon.

VI

SUMMARY OF THE ACHIEVEMENT

IT is now more than twenty years since Kurt Jooss made the first ballet which was presented to a public audience; by now his earliest works of the Ballets Jooss have been danced literally thousands of times before audiences in every part of two continents. Few choreographers can ever have reached so many people inside twelve years, yet any attempt to measure now the significance of Kurt Jooss will fail, because we are too close to the time and the scene of his first impact on the world of Dancing.

Only within recent years have we come to see wherein lay the real value of Isadora Duncan's work; she showed that effective theatrical dancing could be produced without reference to the training system of the established method of Ballet. Part of the result of this dance career has been the preparing of dance audiences for the work of all the innovators who, during the years following the fading of her star, applied themselves to contemporary problems of dramatic dancing.

Kurt Jooss has created a dance method based on a fresh ideology which does not dismiss as artificial the rigorousness and the traditionalism of the Classical Ballet. He has disagreed with that method's idea-basis and has insisted that the conventions grown upon it, chiefly since the days of Noverre, have limited its usefulness for certain purposes. By introducing dance drama in this century he has proved not only that a dramatic form of dancing can be based on a freer form of movement than the Classical system allows, but has shown that this form is immediately theatrically successful, in the age of the Classical Ballet's greatest popularity. It cannot be too strongly stated that the single factor of greatest importance in his career has been the completely detached viewpoint from which he has worked. He has known none of the hindrances to thought and action which a tradition so often imposes on the subconscious processes of the artist. Coming to his study of the Classical Ballet when he was adult, and could make objective analysis of the laws, customs and conventions supporting it, he could remain detached from it. Detached, he could perceive both the real usefulness of its primary principles and the overgrowths of tradition which, in practice, concealed half

77

that usefulness. From the method he appropriated certain elements which he has used for quite different ends from those indicated in the traditional canon.

His method shows now in his workings of the first adaptation of the raw material. This has been assembled under the pressure of experiments with a hundred artistic, psychological, historic and scientific formulas. The guiding rules derived by this means are the substructure of the most individual manifestation of Dancing to be seen to-day. The speculations of Laban ranged over historical and technical variations in the differing forms of the chief European cultures, and after certain examinations of the Platonic teachings, he closely studied Plato's synthesising of the concept of the harmony of the cosmos, and the numerical relations existing between all parts of Nature. From twenty years' study of everything applicable to ideas of Motion, Harmony, Number, Laban had a sufficiency of hypothesis material out of which he could adumbrate certain principles. These formulated principles could be tested by trial and error methods until one or more of them resolved out into a law governing some aspect of harmonised physical movement. Jooss's unique contribution at this stage was to bring a strong sense of the theatre into conjunction with these studies, and he took out what was of value for dealing with the problems of dance-drama. Imaginatively worked upon by means of experimental dances and exercises this material yielded ultimately the basis of rules upon which the whole Jooss system stands. With his creative gift as a choreographer, Jooss allies this other creative faculty : the ability to make formulations which complete the projected hypothesis. Jooss shows that the hypothesis works because he can see how to develop the idea from adumbration to realisation.

In his work Kurt Jooss has had happy collaboration from the earliest days. Dance experimentalism of a novel character needs sympathetic and able collaborators of many kinds, and there have been fellow-artists who saw eye to eye with Jooss from the beginning of his career.

Sigurd Leeder was another pupil of Laban during the Hamburg days, and the alliance between him and Jooss has produced results of the highest value to this system. For Leeder has quite exceptional abilities as a teacher ; besides his mastery of the training and teaching method which he has helped to create, his vast dancing experience helps him to appreciate the dancer's problems, show him how far he can adjust them for himself, and enables him to guide the dancer in overcoming those difficulties. His is the invention of the series of dance studies used as the chief exercise pattern. His ability as a choreographer has mainly been directed on to works which were the final testing of dancers in the Jooss-Leeder school, and recently he has contributed his first ballet to the company's repertory and has further works in preparation.

Frederick Cohen worked as concentratedly upon the special musical problems of the Jooss ballets as their creator did on the choreographic problems. He saw the necessity for " thinking music " in the same way that the choreographer was " thinking dancing " ; the composer's business was to transmute the rhythm of movement into musical rhythm, and to do so in a way that facilitated the work of the dancer. The dramatic expression implies a necessity for expressing precisely, with the musical means, the exactness and brevity of the gesture. Choreographer and composer must between them effect absolute agreement of choreographic and musical forms. He composed for four of the big Jooss ballets—" The Green Table," " The Prodigal Son," " The Mirror " and " A Spring Tale "—and arranged and adapted music for the majority of the other ballets before changing the direction of his musical career after an alliance lasting over sixteen years.

Hein Heckroth had been a colleague from the earliest days ; he is a practically trained man of the Theatre who knows theatre decoration and stagecraft in the degree that Kurt Jooss knows dancing. He designed five of the Jooss ballets still existing, and his contribution has been to project a freshly imagined symbolism by means of dress and staging which matched exactly the symbolic weight given to the drama by Jooss. This ability has been particularly marked in his designing of women's dress ; amongst his other stage and film work he has designed the first large-scale commercial production with projected scenery, " War and Peace." He has probably the best developed sense of the æsthetic and dramatic potentiality of stage lighting amongst designers to-day.

The collaborator whose part in the work is the least obvious is Aino Siimola (now the wife of Kurt Jooss), yet her contribution to the system is implicit in every ballet. She is a co-creator with Jooss, bringing to the final shaping of

78

dance and incident a sense of visual form to complement his strong rhythmic sense. Their two contributions are so knit together that it would be impossible to define exactly what Siimola, and what Jooss, has put into, say, the ballroom sequences of " The Big City " or the diplomats scenes in " The Green Table." In a similar way Jooss and Leeder have both worked upon one another, each giving some gift he had in abundance to the common pooling of their different experiences, backgrounds and sensibilities. There has been, in fact, enormous luck among the collaborators; the right people all came together at the beginning with Jooss—Siimola, Cohen, Leeder, Heckroth—with marked differences of interests yet with each one capable of supplementing the personalities of the others for the common good.

To this brief list of tried friends and worthy colleagues should be added the names of practically every dancer who has ever worked for Jooss, for few have fallen by the way, and the way has been by no means easy. Dancers in Jooss ballets have undertaken a training and rehearsal process quite different from those of any other existing system. They have come from every kind of Classical Ballet background and from all forms of Modern Dance; a good many of those emerging within recent years are entirely products of the Jooss-Leeder school. Male dancers of the highest quality, with great gifts of intelligence, physique and good looks, have been, proportionately, more in evidence in this organisation than in any other Ballet company of our time. Stalwarts such as Rudolf Pescht, Ernst Uthoff, Hans Gansert, Otto Struller and, amongst the women, Elsa Kahl, Aino Siimola, Noelle de Mosa, Ulla Soederbaum, Marja Fedro, have created and danced most of the roles in all the Jooss ballets for years. Many of these dancers, through the misadventures of the past six years, are missing from the Jooss ranks to-day. Yet their pioneer strength and sincerity are matched by an equal integration of abilities among the more recently developed dancers. Hans Zullig has a place in the very top rank of male dancers seen inside twenty years; his unforgettable characterisations of the Simple Young Man in " The Big City," the Prince in " A Spring Tale," and the Youth in " Pandora " show the purest contemporary manifestation of the art of silent drama. With him, Rolf Alexander and Sigurd Leeder form a trio of executants who can compass the whole range of the Jooss repertory. Their feminine parallels, Noelle de Mosa and Ulla Soederbaum, are also dancers come to power within the past few years.

To define their contributions to these works in which the roles have been created by a method of " co-operative choreography " can only be attempted in a document recording and analysing the technical progress through twenty years; a document which theatrical necessity will one day call forth. From amongst these dancers will come the first group of choreographers in the Jooss system—they are, in fact, already emerging. The second and, perhaps, most exciting flowering from the seeds he has sown will be the catalogue of ballets created by the first group of his disciples. No conditions exist which would hinder a choreographer already practised in the Classical Ballet system from essaying a new sort of Ballet on the dancers of this company. For it is precisely through the way in which the best of both systems can be merged in a new sort of choreographic structure, that the two forms can reveal their obviously com-

plementary nature. The Classical Ballet is one side of the whole rich scale of dance-expression; that it should be related to the other side, the dramatic dance of Jooss, is not only desirable, but, under the pressure of Time, inevitable.

Through the skill displayed by the new choreographers, whether emanating from a Jooss school or a Classical academy, in learning and re-projecting all that can be taught from both systems, there can be developed a style of Ballet which will form the Synthesis derivable out of the Thesis of Classicism and the Antithesis of Ballets Jooss. The interim period, extending through twenty or more years, should show the later works of Jooss beside the first ballets of half-a-dozen younger choreographers. If works with the integration and dramatic power of " The Green Table," " The Big City " and " Pandora " can be achieved, on any kind of subject-matter, it seems likely that ideas about Content will have considerable weight in the whole sphere of twentieth century theatrical dancing.

Too many factors are shaping the future of theatrical dancing, and none can foretell its strength or weakness ten years hence. If Ballet still exists as a separate form it will be partly because of what Jooss has done and taught: and perhaps by the end of our century some historian will have weighed to a nicety the importance of Kurt Jooss, and his successors, in the method of the New Ballet.

ON DANCE NOTATION

DURING the same period when Kurt Jooss and his Group were evolving, step by step, the educative and artistic activity which became the workshop and vehicle of the New Ballet, and which on the way—Münster—Essen—Dartington Hall—slowly grew into what is known to-day as the "Jooss-Leeder School of Dance" and "Ballets Jooss"—another development was in progress, and bore fruit in the circle of R. von Laban and his disciples which probably will have a slower but not less profound effect on the further evolution of Ballet Art ; the creation and perfection of the "Kinetography Laban," which, in an entirely new way, tackled and obviously solved the old problem of Dance Notation.

There are indications that attempts towards some form of notation of Dance movement have been made at all times when choreographic compositions have been created. Since the beginnings of what one understands as Ballet Art in Europe, the first essential contribution to Dance Notation was made by the strange French Abbé who called himself Arbeau Thoinôt. In his "Orchesographie" we find a primitive but remarkable attempt to note the elementary step movements of current dances of the time like Branles, Gaillardes, etc., by symbols borrowed from musical notation. Our Plate I shows another primitive way of notation for a ballet on horseback which was part of "Il Mondo Festigiante," a big show given for a Ducal Wedding in Florence in 1661. Whereas Arbeau gives a primitive record with his musical signs of certain forms of steps, the Florentine notation indicates, in a similarly primitive way, the positions on the floor as occupied by different individuals during the dance.

Feuillet whose "Chorégraphie" was published in 1701 used a new method, combining the two principles. Upon a square which—on a small scale—represents the Dance floor, Feuillet draws a continuous line representing the way the dancer is to take, and right and left of this line we find signs for the exact movements which the right or left leg is to perform at the respective place on the dance floor. The music to which it is linked is written across the top of the page (Plate II). Feuillet being a member of Louis XIV's famous "Académie de la Danse" has worked out his signs with scientific accuracy in the observation of the basic movements which build a "step." However he indicates no rhythm for the flow of movement but leaves it to the dancer to adjust his movements according to the duration and character of the music. Also no indication is given for the movements of the torso, head or arms. These are either conventional or left to the discretion of the dancer. There were a number of other systems of dance notation during the 19th Century, all more or less modifications of Feuillet's basic work. But neither Feuillet's nor any of the other methods has proved popular because none was simple enough to be readily readable and yet complete. Noverre dismissed Feuillet's invention as clumsy and unworkable, yet, alas, of Noverre's works only the shadow of shadows has come down to us, whereas the choreographic compositions of Feuillet and Pécourt, as recorded in Feuillet's "Chorégraphie" are there for all time, difficult to decipher but quite possible to reconstruct.

Laban already in his early days felt very strongly about this necessity of a workable system of Dance Notation comparable in simplicity and accuracy to that admirable achievement of combined artistic and intellectual effort which we have to-day in our system of musical notation. His profound studies of the essential elements of movement, rhythmical qualities and harmonious implications—as far as absolute space directions and their relations to the human body are concerned—have enabled him to devise a system of notation based on completely new principles and, as far as its development to date shows, capable of recording each essential detail of rhythmical movement with complete accuracy and yet simple and clear enough to be comfortably writable and readable. Laban's personal efforts were eagerly taken up in his circle of disciples and collaborators, and the "Kinetography Laban" as first published at the Dance Congress at Essen in 1928 was the result of this joint effort of which the main exponents were, besides Laban himself, Kurt Jooss, Sigurd Leeder, Albrecht Knust and Dussia Bereska.

The script system has since been continuously revised and improved while it was taught to hundreds of students on the Continent and at the Jooss-Leeder School at Dartington Hall. It has been successfully introduced to America while in Germany under Nazi ban it went "underground." A great number of Dances and complete ballets has been recorded in "Kinetography" which as a system of notation proved equally competent for works of either classical or modern character. Plate III shows a few bars of the kinetographic score of the "Gentlemen in Black," the first scene of Kurt Jooss's "Green Table." Each system of vertical lines represents one individual dancer. Right and left of the centre line stands for the right or left side of the dancer. Legs, Arms, Torso, Head, etc., have their particular places in the lines. The script is read from the bottom of the page ; all that is found on the same horizontal line is happening at the same time and the duration of a movement is precisely indicated by the height of its sign.

A frequent suggestion in our days is to record a Dance or a Ballet by means of filming it, but it would be impossible to reconstruct a ballet from a film ; just as impossible as it would be for a conductor without a musical score to rehearse even a simple piece of music with his orchestra from a gramophone record.

The history of Music would be unthinkable without the existence of musical notation. A similarly significant development may be expected for the Art of Choreography by a competent and generally practical Dance Notation.

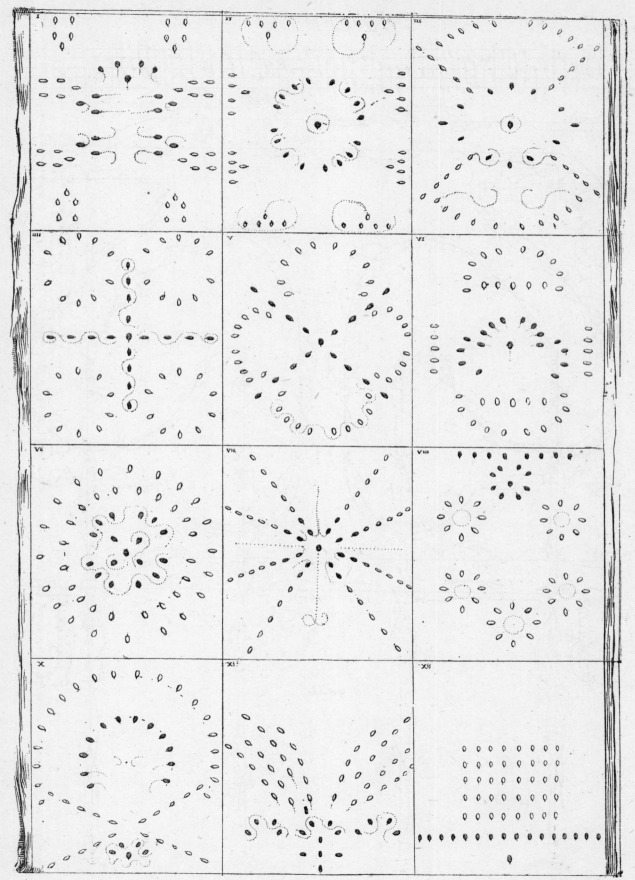

Balet

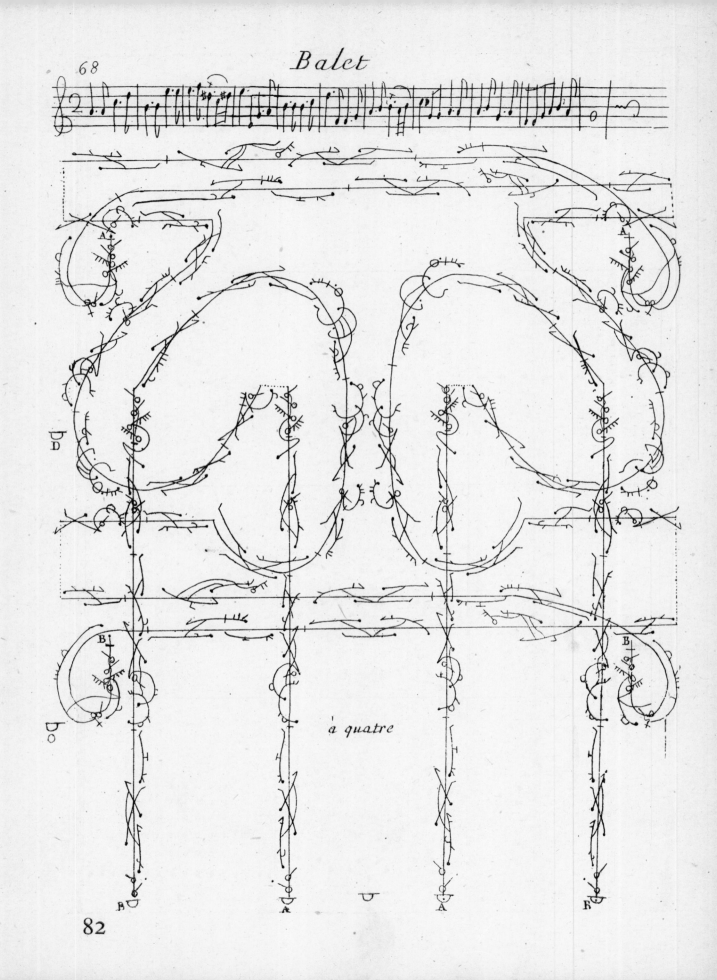

à quatre

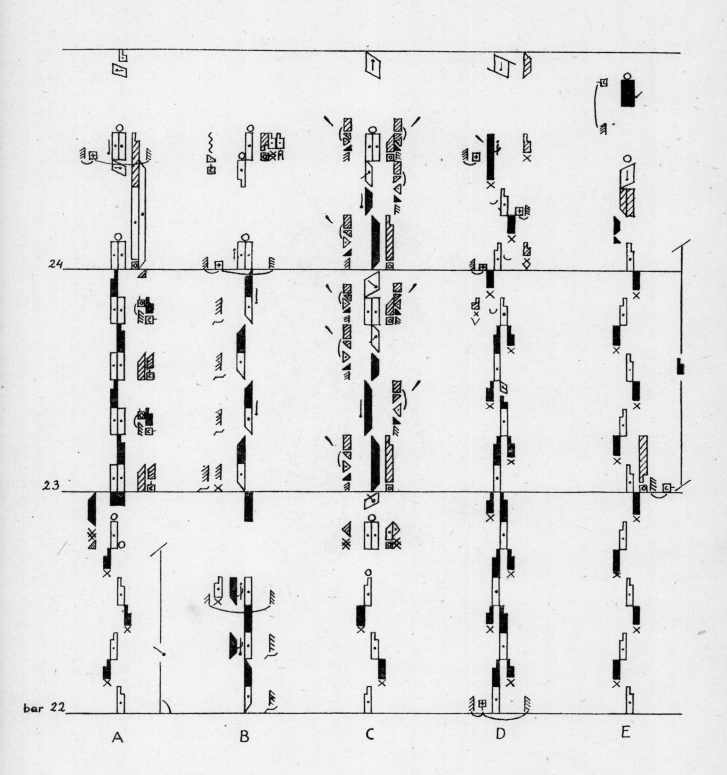

24

23

bar 22

A   B   C   D   E

Kurt Jooss, 1946

H. Heidelsberger

Kurt Jooss and Rudolf Laban with an Icosahedron and Dance Script, Dartington 1939

Fritz Cohen   *Pécsi*

Sigurd Leeder   *Baron*

Aino Siimola   *Anthony*

Hein Heckroth   *Beiny*

Masks by Sigurd Leeder for a projected Dance of Death   Münster 1927

DIE BRAUTFAHRT   Wood Scene   Münster 1925

LARVEN   A duo   Münster 1925

SUITE 1929   Essen 1929

Polovtsian Dances from PRINCE IGOR   Essen 1930

PULCINELLA   Essen 1932

Two Scenes from GROTESKE, a sketch without music
Münster 1927

Students rehearsing at Open Air Theatre, Dartington 1935

Charles E. Brown

Students rehearsing at Open Air Theatre, Dartington 1935

Charles E. Brown

GREEN TABLE   Gentlemen in Black   Paris 1933

Roger Wood

GREEN TABLE Kurt Jooss and Frida Holst as Death and the Old Mother Paris 1932

Lipnitzki

GREEN TABLE   Rudolf Pescht and Otto Struller as Death and the Profiteer   Dartington 1936

Anthony

GREEN TABLE   Gentlemen in Black   Essen 1932   *Renger-Patsch*

THE BIG CITY   Street Scene   Budapest 1937

Pécsi

THE BIG CITY   The Workers' Quarter   Noelle de Mosa and Ernst Uthoff   Dartington 1935   *Anthony*

THE BIG CITY   The Workers' Quarter   Gabor Cossa, Elsa Kahl, and Herta Thiele   Dartington 1935   *Anthony*

THE BIG CITY   The Workers' Quarter   Budapest 1937   *Pécsi*

THE BIG CITY   The Workers' Quarter   Amsterdam 1935   *Kahle*

Kahle

THE BIG CITY   The
Workers'   Quarter
Amsterdam 1935

THE BIG CITY   The Dance Hall   Amsterdam 1935   *Kahle*

THE BIG CITY   Street Scene   Hans Zullig   Amsterdam 1935   *Kahle*

A BALL IN OLD VIENNA   Karl Bergeest as the Dancing Master   Essen 1932

Kurt Jooss

A BALL IN OLD VIENNA Amsterdam 1934   *Kahle*

A BALL IN OLD VIENNA   London 1945

Roger Wood

A BALL IN OLD VIENNA   London 1945

Roger Wood

PAVANE Paris 1933   *Lipnitzki*

PAVANE Essen 1929   *Sigurd Leeder*

Hans Zullig and Noelle de Mosa in BALLADE   London 1935

Anthony

BALLADE   Budapest 1937   *Pécsi*

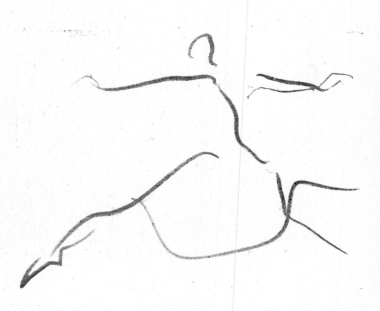

BALLADE Budapest 1937   *Pécsi*

THE MIRROR Gambling Scene Dartington 1935   *Anthony*

THE MIRROR   The Unemployed   Amsterdam 1935   *Kahle*

Otto Struller and Elsa Kahl in JOHANN STRAUSS TONIGHT   London 1935

JOHANN STRAUSS TONIGHT London 1935   *Anthony*

SEVEN HEROES   Scene One in first production   Paris 1934   *Lipnitzki*

SEVEN HEROES   Ulla Soederbaum as the Innkeeper's Daughter   New York 1938   *Fritz Henle*

SEVEN HEROES First Scene New York 1938

Fritz Henle

SEVEN
HEROES
Second
Scene
London 1945

Roger Wood

SEVEN
HEROES
First Scene
Cambridge
1945

Dennis Dobson

CHRONICA   Death of Filippo   Dartington 1939   *Baron*

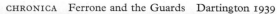

CHRONICA   Ferrone and the Guards   Dartington 1939   *Baron*

Ulla Soederbaum and Hans Zullig in A SPRING TALE   London 1939

Anthony

A SPRING TALE   Hans Zullig, Elsa Kahl, and Ulla Soederbaum   London 1939

A SPRING TALE   Final Scene   Dartington 1939

PRODIGAL SON   The Tyrant   Rolf Alexander   London 1945

PRODIGAL SON   The Seductress   Hans Zullig, Florence Reed, and Rolf Alexander   London 1945

Roger Wood

PRODIGAL SON The Return London 1945

PRODIGAL SON The Return Kurt Jooss, Maria Fedro, and Rolf Alexander London 1945

COMPANY AT THE MANOR   Patricia Clogstoun, Jack Skinner, and Audrey Seed   Liverpool 1943

Tunbridge-Sedgwick

COMPANY AT THE MANOR   Rolf Alexander and Noelle de   *Lee*
                        Mosa   Bath 1943

COMPANY AT THE MANOR Noelle
de Mosa and Hans Zullig   London
1944

Dennis Dobson

COMPANY AT THE MANOR   Hans Zullig and Ulla Soederbaum   London 1944

Picture Post

PANDORA Part
One The Strong
Man and the Go-
getter London
1944

Picture Post

PANDORA Part
One, Pandora and
the Go-getter
London 1944

Picture Post

PANDORA   Part One   Noelle de Mosa, Sigurd Leeder, and Rolf Alexander   London 1944   *Edward Mandinian*

PANDORA   Part One   Final Scene : The Crowning of Pandora   London 1944   *Edward Mandinian*

PANDORA   Ulla Soederbaum and Hans Zullig as Psyche and the Youth   London 1944

Picture Post

PANDORA   Part Two   London 1944

Edward Mandinian

PANDORA   Part Two   London 1944   *Edward Mandinian*

PANDORA Part Two London 1944

Edward Mandinian

Maria Fedro as The Mother in the Final
Scene of PANDORA London 1944 ⟫⟫

Lee Miller

SAILOR'S FANCY Scene One Joy
Bolton-Carter and Rolf Alexander
Bath 1943

Lee Miller

SAILOR'S FANCY   Scene Two   Noelle de Mosa and
Sigurd Leeder Bath 1943

Lee Miller

SAILOR'S FANCY   Scene Three   Hans Zullig, Sigurd Leeder, and Rolf Alexander   Bath 1943

Lee Miller

SAILOR'S FANCY   Scene Three   Hans Zullig and Ulla Soederbaum   Bath 1943   *Lee Miller*

SAILOR'S FANCY Scene Four
Bath 1943

Lee Miller

SAILOR'S FANCY Last Scene
Bath 1943

Lee Miller

SAILOR'S FANCY · Last Scene · Bath 1943   *Lee Miller*

Noelle de Mosa and Hans Zullig in LE BOSQUET   London 1945

LE BOSQUET   London 1945   *Roger Wood*

LE BOSQUET Cambridge 1945

LE BOSQUET   Noelle de Mosa   London 1945   *Roger Wood*

NOTES

1. The most important figures in Ballet are the choreographers, the creative artists who correspond, in the sphere of music, with composers. Without the composer, whatever his stature, there is neither Opera, Symphony, Suite nor Concerto ; so with Ballet, without the accumulated pedagogy and creative achievements of the great choreographers and dance-teachers, there is nothing for the Pavlovas, the Karsavinas, the Markovas to dance.

Coralli was one of the outstanding choreographers of the Romantic period (ca. 1815-45) : Petipa and Ivanov later in the century reshaped the Romantic ideology and gave this Neo-Romanticism its perfect expression in " Le Lac des Cygnes " (1892). Fokine (1880-1943) is one of the great historical personages in all Ballet : two master-pieces of a quality unlike anything we have inherited from earlier days, " Les Sylphides " and " Petrouchka," will outwear all the rest of his achievement. Each of these represents in a unique way the efflorescence of a certain appraisal of choreographic art that can never be repeated. After Fokine, the choreographers Nijinsky, Massine, Nijinska and Balanchine carried forward the creative strain in the Diaghilev organisation : each of them was the ultimate product of the Russian Imperial Academy and Theatres system, Balanchine having seven years' choreographic and dancing experience in the Soviet system (1917-24). Tudor, with wonderfully co-ordinated dancing and musical " atmospherics," exploits the comparatively new field (for Ballet) of the psycho-analytical revelation of character : he is not only the outstanding figure of the English renaissance of Ballet, but, amongst Classical Ballet choreographers, the figure of next importance in Ballet to-day following on the five Diaghilev masters noted above.

2. After Diaghilev's death in August 1929, his company disintegrated, and the choreographers and dancers scattered to the theatres of Scandinavia, Italy, South America, the United States, etc. Mostly, wherever they worked, they reproduced some of the aura of the Diaghilev system ; discipline in preparation, precision in dance-style, efficiency in the staging of productions with which they were associated. They had come from working in the best company of the Golden Age of Ballet, and so could not avoid spreading some of the excellencies of method (however diluted) which were part of the Diaghilev signature. When new organisations came into existence in the early 1930's, to pursue the promotion of big-scale Ballet, these choreographers and dancers became an indispensable adjunct to the various impresarios, and, in fact, filled most places in the higher ranks of dancers and were also the choreographers of the resurgence.

3. The academic training of dancers and the subsequent provision of careers within the Imperial Theatres system, in Russia, was of the highest pedagogic excellence and developed the most refined sort of executant. But the dancers used their gifts in elaborate, overdressed, fussily staged and unimaginatively orchestrated ballets of an unbelievable poverty of idea. This was inevitable when one reflects that the Ballet was a Court entertainment in the most rigorously controlled police state in the world. Ballet had to be " safe," avoiding all contact with the real world even through any sort of symbolism. By the time of Fokine it had degenerated into a mechanism enabling ballerinas to display their favourite " specialty numbers." The formulas for plot were well-worn Greek, Roman and mediæval legends, and hopelessly out-of-date Romantic themes which had had some validity sixty years previously, but by 1900 were anachronisms.

That strong theatrical leaning which is part of the Russian character, and the desire of those in authority to pre-serve intact the whole educational apparatus even during the chaos of revolution, were the reasons for the Soviet Government maintaining the Imperial Theatres system uninterruptedly from 1917 on. No widespread admiration existed for Russian Ballet in Russia, and the ideology behind Ballet has undergone some startling changes since 1917, but they are probably not as dynamic as the changes we have seen in the Western world since Diaghilev's heyday. No useful comparisons or estimations can be made until companies of Soviet dancers appear with their contemporary ballets in theatres outside Russia.

4. Vigano, who immediately preceded the Romantic period of Ballet, is a landmark in the history of the art ; probably the first *great* choreographer, for he followed the precepts of Noverre, and made for himself conditions within which he could produce ballets of quality. He achieved success by working with passion and imagination for the harmonious welding together of Music, Mime and Dance. He may be claimed to have created the first real ballets (i.e., theatrical spectacles which had dramatic as well as visual attraction), for even Noverre, who first made the action in Ballet progressive, worked within a conventional series of plots and themes, and was, therefore, to some extent, limited in inventiveness. Vigano's great creative period was 1800-20 ; he died in the latter year.

5. Arbeau and Beauchamps, French dancing masters of the sixteenth and seventeenth centuries, and Carlo Blasis, an Italian of the early nineteenth century, are the key figures in the pedagogic delineation of the Classical Ballet method. Each at his time was representative of the most complete formulations about the teaching of this dance method, which has undergone steady technical improvement for three hundred years, culminating in the " Russian style " of training which is to-day taught through Cecchetti's method.

6. Epidauros was the site of one of the largest, and reputedly most beautiful, Greek open-air theatres : a crowd of over fifteen thousand could be accommodated on its fifty-four semi-circular banks of seats. At the time it was in use, a Theatre was still very much a Temple ; the play-acting and play-watching were a serious and fascinating way of observing one's duty to the gods, and the emotional temperature of the gatherings was a good deal higher than we are accustomed to experience to-day in the Theatre.

7. This very brief résumé of only the principal lines of Platonic thought along which Laban and Jooss have worked for many years, seems at this point a sufficient comment on the sources of the Jooss method. A more closely developed study of the macrocosm-microcosm relationship, and of the Delsartean formulations on Gesture, must preface the first teaching manual of the Jooss dance and choreography—whenever that may be written. The dance-student who is inclined towards stimulating reading will find some of the basic material of Jooss's works and philosophy in " Plato's Cosmology " (a translation, with commentary, of " The Timæus," by F. M. Cornford) and " Crystals : Secrets of the Inorganic," by J. Killian. There are some striking deductions, worthy of comparison with the conventional art-histories, in Spengler's " Decline of the West," particularly Vol. I, chapters 2, 7 and 8. Adolphe Appia published his two works in French and German ; they comprise his theorisings on Plasticity and Emotional Projection, and reveal an interesting viewpoint on problems which are the concern of all choreographers and producers of movement. They form a valuable, though as yet little appreciated, part of that European literature which embodies the past fifty years' cerebration on the Theatre. The works of Rudolf Laban await translation into English. The best of his practical application (before the years of the Laban-Jooss association) is in " Choregraphie " (Diederichs, Jena, 1926).

8. Prince Serge Wolkonsky, the last Intendant of the Imperial Theatre in Petersburg, was an associate of Diaghilev when the latter worked, for a while, in the Imperial Theatre system before founding his own organisation. Wolkonsky's introduction of Delsarte's method to the Russian academies has taken root, and some species of Delsartean gestural training is part of the curriculum in the principal Soviet academies to-day.

9. These two films were the earliest attempts (both highly successful) at reproducing the contemporary scene as filmic subject-matter in its own right. Each brilliantly revealed the integration of its director with his subject-matter : in " Rien que les heures " Cavalcanti elevated the commonplace of the Parisian streets on to the plane of the poetic, and Ruttmann projected the " spirit " of the Berlin of that time through highly symbolic, mechanistic images. The latter film was notably influenced by the novel cutting methods then being brought into use by such Russian masters as Dziga-Vertov and Pudovkin. Hundreds of documentaries since carry a faint though still perceptible impress of the signatures of Cavalcanti and Ruttmann.

10. *Kitsch*—this is to-day an indispensable word in the vocabularies of those who look at contemporary Western culture with clear eyes. I have not come across any better appreciation of this phenomenon than that which occurs in Clement Greenberg's essay in " Horizon " (Vol. I, No. 4, April 1940) where he describes the thing and its genesis in these words : " . . . That thing to which the Germans give the wonderful name of kitsch ; popular commercial art and literature with their chromeotypes, magazine covers, illustrations, ads., slick and pulp fiction, comics, Tin Pan Alley music, tap dancing, Hollywood movies, etc. Kitsch is the product of the Industrial Revolution which urbanised the masses of Western Europe and America and established what is called universal literacy. . . . The peasants who settled in the cities as proletariat and petty bourgeois learned to read and write for the sake of efficiency, but they did not win the leisure and comfort necessary for the enjoyment of the city's traditional culture. Discovering a new capacity for boredom at the same time, the new urban masses set up a pressure on society to provide them with a kind of culture fit for their own consumption. A new commodity was devised, ersatz culture, kitsch, destined for those who, insensible to the values of real culture, are hungry nevertheless for the diversion that only culture of some sort can provide. Kitsch, using for raw material the debased and academicised simulacra of genuine culture, welcomes and cultivates this insensibility. Kitsch is mechanical and operates by formulas. Kitsch is vicarious experience and faked sensations. Kitsch changes according to style, but remains always the same. Kitsch is the epitome of all that is spurious in the life of our times. Kitsch pretends to demand nothing of its customers except their money—not even their time."

NOTES ON SOME BALLETS REFERRED TO IN THE TEXT

GISELLE (1841). Choreography by Coralli and Perrot; music of A. Adam. The oldest ballet in continuous repertory since its creation; within the conventions of its sort, a choreographic masterpiece in which all the action flows from the plot, and, with the exception of short mime " conversations," is *danced*. The principal role demands acting and dancing ability of a super-normal order, and is the European Theatre's " female Hamlet." To-day the work is danced by Soviet Russian, European and American ballet companies.

LE LAC DES CYGNES (1895). Choreography by Petipa and Ivanov; music of Tchaikovsky. Romantic-subject ballets, of which " Giselle " is the prototype, gave way to ballets based on adventure stories and melodrama. The corps-de-ballet ceased to be nereids, pixies and wilis and were now garbed and identified as houris, milkmaids, slaves or gypsies. The stories (as recorded in Cyril Beaumont's invaluable catalogue : " The Complete Book of Ballets ") suggest a charming naïveté shared equally by choreographer and audience. This type, with few exceptions, remained the balletic norm up to Fokine's day. The major exception is " Le Lac des Cygnes."
Petipa discovered the music after Tchaikovsky's death (1893) and with his lieutenant Ivanov created this master-piece. It is an artistically proportioned work with music, choreography and libretto fully co-ordinated; a romantic tragedy on a theme dating from the dawn of our civilisation, the metamorphosis of woman into bird. The sheer inventions of dance and miming give it unique artistic, as well as historic, importance.

LES SYLPHIDES (1908). Choreography by Fokine; music of Chopin. In this ballet Fokine established as a norm for choreographic procedure what Petipa and Ivanov had, almost incidentally, done in " Le Lac des Cygnes " : he invented dance movements which gave visual shape to the lyrical evocations of the musical score. There is neither story, time, place, hero nor heroine; it is the undiluted essence of the classic dance system as developed up to Fokine's day (1908), stylistically focused in an imagined reminiscence of Taglioni's manner in " La Sylphide " (1832). No one else has arranged a ballet in the nineteenth century classic mode, of the same order of abstraction, and with such a wealth of choreographic invention.

PETROUCHKA (1911). Choreography by Fokine; music of Stravinsky; libretto by Stravinsky and Benois. Fokine's characters of Petrouchka, The Doll and The Blackamoor have dramatic integrity because of the completely choreographic method by which they are brought to life and enact their tragic tale. They have also an inescapable symbolic significance as three constantly occurring types in European legend and lore : The Innocent who suffers because of his lack of worldly wisdom, The Woman who amuses herself with him but refuses his genuine affection, and The Realist who profits by the stupidity and innocence of these two. In a period of intense choreographic reformation, this work was notable for its unifying of music, theme, dance and decor, and is a magnificent artistic achievement comparable with " Les Sylphides."

ODE (1928). Choreography by Massine; libretto of Kochno (after Lomonosov); music of Nabokov; decor and lighting by Tchelitchev and Charbonnier. Nominally created to expound Lomonosov's pantheistic parable, this ballet is important for the new technical and expressionistic freedoms which Massine established. His well-knit choreography and masterly experimenting with lighting, symbolic decor and furnishings and simplified costume, made a complete breakaway from the basic twentieth century one-act archetypes fixed by Fokine and Nijinsky. Most of the important designing, staging and lighting innovations in classical Ballet practice since 1930 can be referred back to this production.

COTILLON (1932). Choreography by Balanchine; music of Chabrier. This ballet is the perfect flowering of one aspect of Balanchine's genius—the ability to devise dance-images from the inner core of musical thought expressed through the score. This imagery is of great visual beauty and is laden with symbolic implication. Beside a fine performance of one of his best works (Apollo Musagetes, Le Fils Prodigue, Cotillon) the works of most other choreo-graphers have the obviousness of the parade ground in their simple geometric evolutions. His works are visual orchestrations, on moving bodies, which parallel the fine texture of the music's orchestral form.

CHOREARTIUM (1933). Choreography by Massine; music of Brahms (4th Symphony). This work breaks clear away from every established convention of twentieth century ballet-making; it is an attempt—mostly successful in my opinion—to build a visual dancing counterpart to the aural patterning of Brahms's symphony. No recognisable story, scenario, characterisation, time, place, nor period is drawn upon : dancers move in three-dimensional space creating dance-images partly inspired by, related to, and extending beyond the normal responses evoked by the score, as heard in concert performances. Because it established a new kind of expressionistic freedom, the work is as important historically as " Le Lac des Cygnes," " Les Sylphides " and " Petrouchka."

HOROSCOPE (1938). Choreography by Frederick Ashton; music of Constant Lambert. Ashton's first work on a basis of idea as large as any used by Massine; in which the co-ordination of libretto, music, decor and choreo-graphy was of a perfection seen in not more than half-a-dozen contemporary ballets—by any choreographer. This work and some ballets by Tudor showed that choreographic development of English Ballet since its rebirth was justly comparable with the choreographic growth shown in any ballet-making system in the Western world.

152

THE BALLETS OF KURT JOOSS

and other ballets existing in the repertory of the Ballets Jooss

Ballet	Music	Designer	Date	Group or Company	Theatre and City
A Persian Ballet	Egon Wellesz	Hein Heckroth	July 1924	Neue Tanzbühne	International Festival of Modern Music, Donaueschingen
Der Dämon	Paul Hindemith	,, ,,	March 1925	,, ,,	Theater der Stadt Münster
Die Brautfahrt	Rameau, Couperin et Al.	,, ,,	May 1925	,, ,,	,, ,, ,,
Larven	Percussion by Jooss	,, ,,	October 1925	,, ,,	,, ,, ,,
Tragödie	Frederick A. Cohen	,, ,,	May 1926	,, ,,	,, ,, ,,
Kaschemme	,, ,,	,, ,,	October 1926	,, ,,	,, ,, ,,
Drosselbart	Mozart	,, ,,	March 1929	Folkwang Tanztheater Studio	Opera House, Essen
Room 13	F. A. Cohen	,, ,,	October 1929	,, ,,	,, ,, ,,
Suite 1929	,, ,,	,, ,,	October 1929	,, ,,	,, ,, ,,
Pavane	Ravel	Sigurd Leeder	October 1929	,, ,,	,, ,, ,,
Petrouchka	Stravinsky	Hein Heckroth	February 1930	,, ,,	,, ,, ,,
Gaukelei	F. A. Cohen	Hermann Haertlein	2 May 1930	,, ,,	,, ,, ,,
Le Bal	Vittorio Rieti	Hein Heckroth	November 1930	Folkwang Tanzbühne, Essen	,, ,, ,,
Danses Polovtsiennes	Borodin	,, ,,	November 1930	,, ,,	,, ,, ,,
Coppelia	Delibes	,, ,,	25 February 1931	,, ,,	,, ,, ,,
Fils Prodigue	Prokofiev	,, ,,	28 May 1931	,, ,,	,, ,, ,,
Pulcinella	Stravinsky	,, ,,	April 1932	,, ,,	,, ,, ,,
The Green Table	F. A. Cohen	,, ,,	3 July 1932	,, ,,	Theatre des Champs-Elysées, Paris
The Big City	Alexandre Tansman	,, ,,	21 November 1932	,, ,,	Opera House, Cologne
A Ball in Old Vienna	Joseph Lanner (Arranged by F. A. Cohen)	Aino Siimola	21 November 1932	,, ,,	,, ,,
Seven Heroes	Purcell (Arranged by F. A. Cohen)	Hein Heckroth	1 October 1933	Ballets Jooss	Schouwburg-Maastricht (Holland)
Prodigal Son	F. A. Cohen	,, ,,	6 October 1933	Folkwang Tanzbühne	Stadt-Schouwburg, Amsterdam
Ballade	John Colman	,, ,,	23 September 1935	Ballets Jooss	Opera House, Manchester
The Mirror	F. A. Cohen	,, ,,	28 September 1935	,, ,,	,, ,,
Johann Strauss, To-night !	J. Strauss (Arranged by F. A. Cohen)	Georg Kirsta	21 October 1935	,, ,,	Gaiety Theatre, London
★Seven Heroes	Purcell (Arranged by F. A. Cohen)	Hein Heckroth (New Designs)	9 October 1937	,, ,,	Lyric Theatre, Baltimore, U.S.A.
A Spring Tale	F. A. Cohen	Hein Heckroth	8 February 1939	,, ,,	New Theatre, Oxford
Chronica	Berthold Goldschmidt	Dmitri Bouchène	14 February 1939	,, ,,	Arts Theatre, Cambridge
★Prodigal Son	F. A. Cohen	,, ,,	October 1939	,, ,,	Prince's Theatre, Bristol
Company at the Manor	Beethoven (Arranged by J. Cook)	Doris Zinkeisen	15 February 1943	,, ,,	Arts Theatre, Cambridge
Pandora	Roberto Gerhard	Hein Heckroth	26 January 1944	,, ,,	,, ,,

(Choreography of all the above Ballets by Kurt Jooss)

Ballet	Music	Designer	Date	Group or Company	Theatre and City
Sailors' Fancy (Choreography by Sigurd Leeder)	Martin Penny (Arrangement of Traditional Airs)	Hein Heckroth	16 February 1943	,, ,,	,, ,,
Le Bosquet (Choreography by Hans Zullig)	Rameau (Arranged by Martin Penny)	Doris Zinkeisen	31 January 1945	,, ,,	,, ,,

★ Second production of this work : with new choreography and new costume designs.

INDEX